Stephanie Gladysz

(Gasp)

I Have an Idea!

Playful little stories focused on God's ideas
that have helped make our home
lively and alive
in Christ

(Gasp)
I Have an Idea!

Playful little stories focused on God's ideas
that have helped make our home
lively and alive
in Christ

Stephanie Gladysz

(Gasp) I Have an Idea!
Playful little stories focused on God's ideas
that have helped make our home lively
and alive in Christ
by Stephanie Gladysz

Printed in the United States of America

ISBN 9781613796900

Unless otherwise indicated, Bible quotations are taken from The New American Standard Bible Version of the Bible. Copyright © 1960, 1962, 1963, 1968, 1971, 1972, 1973, 1975, 1977, 1995, 1998 by The Lockman Foundation.

www.xulonpress.com

Dedication

W ithout hesitation, I'm dedicating this little book to the loves of my life- my husband, Ron and our little flock, Genevieve, Alexandra, Jamison and Brooklynne. Even though I can write a book, I can't seem to find words that describe how much I love you all. I pray you'll see it in these pages. I'll put it simply... I love you and thank God for you everyday.

Thank you notes...

Writing a book is a bit like making a scrumptious pot of homemade soup.

It takes time, planning and a whole lot of different ingredients. The warm journey to becoming a hearty soup requires some attention and gentle loving. The soup beckons to be stirred for encouragement and tasted for saltiness, then left to simmer. You can't hurry a good soup. It needs to be carefully seasoned to achieve that soothing comfort food flavour. And then, one more taste test by the friend who's hovering around the kitchen. Making soup involves lots of love. Writing a book involves the love of lots.

Whenever I read a book I take a good look at the acknowledgements. I stand in bookstores gazing at long lists of helpers, marveling at the support people who've worked alongside the author. God knew that when it was my turn, He'd provide for every one of my needs. He's given me an incredible family and loving friends who've cheered me on and loved me through this project. God has truly blessed me. You'll see that shortly.

Mom, you and Dad were always willing to sit for hours listening to my attempts at creative writing. You gave me the opportunity to go to journalism school. Thank you for always loving me and for raising me in a home that was all about family and full of Jesus. Thank you and I love you.

Ron, my sweet husband. Loving? Yes. Patient? Yes. Kind? Yes. Gentle? Yes. Faithful? Yes. Good? Really good. Open to ideas? You sure have been. Just read the book again. Thank you for being my Boaz. I love you lots.

Genevieve, 27 years ago God started a new chapter of this book when life with you began. Amazingly, even as a toddler you showed me Jesus and you continue to point me to Christ daily. Thank you that you love a good idea! You are a woman who is always quick to say "yes" to Jesus.

Alexandra, God uses you to remind me to live life with gusto, while in dependence on Him. He's knitted you together in a unique way. You're a congenial, sensitive and lively woman who shines for Jesus. Thank you for fanning the spark in me to write this book. Christ brings me joy through you.

Jamison, I'm so thankful that God gave us a boy amidst all these girls. Such a good idea. The creativity that God has poured into you motivates me so much. As I've told you many times, I'm thankful you're our son and no one else's. I admire both your quiet strength and the tender heart God's given you. What a combination. Be a Boaz.

Brooklynne, you're the little one. Maybe that's why we have a special bond. I'm so thankful God gave us one more girl. That was another one of His great ideas. Your zest for a life in Christ is irresistible and contagious. You do the best laugh-cry I've ever seen. You make me smile. I love how you love Jesus.

Edna, if we hadn't gotten together for a hot cup of tea on that bitterly cold January afternoon a few years ago, I wonder if I would've had the courage to write a book. God had a good idea to use you to spur me on to write, write, write. Thank you dear friend.

Vicki, God had another great idea when He positioned our homes on the same street. When I first set up my desk at the living room window to write this book, it just seemed like a nice bright place to work. I had no idea that God would use your drive-bys and wild waving to inspire me to remain focused on this task. Thank you, my little friend and creeper. Please don't ever move.

Marlene, you are a wise and gracious woman. I'm one blessed girl to call you my friend. You've answered late night questions and even vacationed with my manuscript. Thank you for your godly input into so many areas of my life.

Sheila, each day I repeat the same thing to the Lord. I thank Him for your editing skills. It's like God reached down over the balconies of heaven and handed me a silver platter loaded with the gift of your love, time, enthusiasm, patience, honesty and friendship. Let's cook up a Mediterranean storm together soon.

Lord. I love you. Thank you for taking charge of every word in this book. But thank you more for the abundant life You've given me in Jesus Christ- it's a daily celebration with You. You alone have the best ideas.

Menu Options

Introduction

The Appetizer

(Gasp) I have an idea! I've probably exclaimed that hundreds of times over the past 30 years. Most of the time as soon as those four little words leave my lips, I can see my husband and children run in five different directions, only to stop and nonchalantly peek back listening with curiosity. They know the announcement of a new idea usually means their involvement in some unusual way. But the children will also admit that God has used these ideas to help mold them into young people who love the Lord Jesus Christ.

Ideas just sort of pop into my head. That's truly the only way I can describe it. And this usually happens when I least expect it. After all, God doesn't always give us a heads-up on the things He's about to do.

Girlfriend, I want you to understand one very important thing, right from page one. If you can't grasp this next idea, then please don't read any further. Put this book down, come back another time and try again.

Not one of the ideas in this book is mine. Every lively story, each inspiring thought and rich Scripture are all God's ideas. Even the recipes tucked in here and there are from the hand of God. Yes, there are recipes too! I'm excited for you to use them to help serve some culinary T.L.C. to your loved ones. All of these gifts come from the creative, wonderful and Almighty God. The Lord Jesus Christ. Are you with me on this? Thank you. You may read on now. Why not make yourself a cup of coffee while you're at it? I can wait a few minutes.

It's the sheer desire of my heart that each word you read will point you to Christ. It's the utmost desire of my heart that God will use this book to inspire you to seek Him and His will for your home. And it's the ultimate desire of my heart that you know that a life in Christ is your greatest need.

You may think that sounds pretty heavy for what you thought was a cute little book of funky ideas for your family and home. This is still the playful book you purchased (or borrowed) and I know the Lord won't let you down.

Writing a book has been "an idea" in my head for... hmm... over a decade. You could say it's one of those things I've been pondering in my heart-to quote some tender, well-written words from my favourite Author.

I've always sensed this book would be a collection of stories focused on God's ideas for our family that have helped to make our home lively and alive in Christ. God stirred my heart to combine His perfect ideas, with the supreme value He places on the family, to be the core of this book. I also realized this all had to be underscored with the Word of God, and so I enthusiastically began to seek Him for those Scriptures. And, of course, He was faithful to guide me through His Word. A life lived in Christ is such an adventure!

Some of the ideas in this book are almost three decades old. Others have popped up in the past few years. I'm as excited about the well-used classic ones, as I am about the newer ones. They're all my favourites!

Warning: You're about to get a very close-up look at our family, but please don't try to make your family look like our family. Sister, that won't work. I've been praying that you will look to Jesus to transform these ideas into what He has for you and your family. Seek Him, abide in Him and wait on Him.

Thanks for spending time with me here in the opening pages of this book. I'm so anxious for you to read on and see Jesus, and how He's worked in our family. After all, He's been putting this book together for 30 years. He has great ideas!

One final thought. You'll read about many wonderful people throughout this book. I want you to know that their names have not been changed. There was no way I would rename the incredible people I love.

One

A Holy Coincidence

**Proverbs 24:3 & 4 By wisdom a house is built,
And by understanding it is established;
And by knowledge the rooms are filled
With all precious and pleasant riches.**

M y idea of an adventure is sensing the Lord stirring His ideas within me, which then become precious and pleasant riches in our home.

That's exactly what happened one glorious spring day in the family room of our home in southwest Calgary, as I was blissfully playing with our first baby, Genevieve. It was while God had me enjoying the ordinary things in life, like stacking blocks with her, that He walked me right into one of His ideas that He would use over the next 27 years to bless and encourage our family.

Our beloved little girl was about to be six months old the very next day. Half a year old! I thought that was monumental. Then it happened. I suddenly had what I call a *(gasp) I have an idea!* moment. I immediately knew that we had to have a celebration, a party. You see, I was a normal young mom, totally in love with, and smitten by our sweet young daughter. It seemed natural that we should have some festivities.

I called my parents and explained the story. I'm quite sure my mother, who was a proud, first-time grandmother, headed straight to her harvest gold kitchen to whip up a torte as soon as she hung up the phone. My next call was to my dear neighbours- young moms who also had baby girls and could share my joy. They agreed to come over the next afternoon, when nap-time was over of course- after all, I wanted the tiny guest of honour to be at her best for her first... in-between birthday celebration. I think I was the happiest mom in Calgary that afternoon.

Since I was a little girl I've loved Jesus, however in those early years of parenthood I was so wrapped up in all the wonderful blessings I enjoyed, that I almost missed Jesus, who was my blessing! But His grace was so gracious and His patience was so patient, that slowly and steadily He showed me I needed to acknowledge Him as my life, and to be more in awe of Him than the blessing. He gently taught me to commit and submit to Him, in all things, at all times... even when it seemed like life was mostly diaper time, feeding time, laundry time, meal time, nap time, grocery time, playtime, swim time, story time... and ahh, bedtime.

And these in-between birthdays... well, if anyone asked any of our four children how old they were, even at a young age, they could respond in a small but confident voice, "two and a half," or "six and three quarters" or "eleven and a quarter." You see, we began to regularly celebrate in-between birthdays on the quarter, half and three quarters.

I can see you doing some quick math in your heads. With four children, that would mean 12 in-between birthday celebrations annually. True. But the magnitude of these birthdays has never been anything like real birthday festivities. Children are a gift from God and we applaud that whenever we can!

Here's a peek at how things would look. Our daughter Alexandra's seven and three quarter birthday was on May 2nd. On that day she may have had the option of inviting a couple of friends over for lunch, or choosing the dinner menu for that night. Or perhaps the children would get a small present as a special treat

Quite often a child wouldn't even realize it was their in-between birthday until I announced it. Their faces would light up as they joyously exclaimed, "it's my in-between birthday?!" As you can imagine, I had to keep track of the dates very closely, but after several years it became natural for me to know each special day. And yes, every month of the year we have a real or in-between celebration.

As they've become older, it's become special to celebrate in-between birthdays across the continent. Now the gifts have become e-cards, text messages, e-mails and phone calls. I still send a small goodie in the mail, perhaps some tea, or a gift card for coffee with a friend. Whatever the Lord suggests. It was His idea to begin with.

Over the years, numerous friends have asked if they could join our family just to get in on this treat, but we've graciously declined. Even recently, Genevieve told me that a good friend, who works with her in Texas, would like to join the family. Sheila, you know we love you- but sorry.

So why all the hoopla? Jesus has commanded us to love one another. And I have truly taken that commandment to heart. To this day I am more in love with all four of our young adult children than ever. I told you I was smitten back then and I still am today.

Unless the Lord leads me to, I can't imagine ever bringing in-between birthdays to a close. He's made these legendary in the Gladysz home. I wonder if our children will one day bring this ritual to their own families? Well, if they don't, praise the Lord, I already have an idea.

Let me add something here. Yesterday, January 24th, I read the theme verses for this book, which are Proverbs 24:3 & 4. And in a "holy coincidence" sort of way, it's also the day I began writing this book. What a gift!

Some in-between birthday celebration ideas...

- let the child choose the meals for the whole day
- wake them up with breakfast in bed
- set a special spot at the table for them
- run a bubble bath for them at bedtime, with candles and music
- give them an envelope with the cutest baby pictures that you can find

- buy them new socks, pajamas or something they need
- let them choose where to sit in the van
- invite some of their friends over after school for popcorn
- go to the library
- play home spa together
- stroll through the hardware store; Jamison loved that one!
- surprise them with a card, text message or e-mail, plus a phone call
- mail them their favourite snack, tea, coffee or old family photos
- send a love note and Bible verse

One more thing... the very first gift we ever gave as an in-between birthday gift was to 6-month-old Genevieve. It was a Fisher Price Rolly Polly Chime Ball. I still have it safely tucked away. And I think I know what I'll do with it someday....

Two

MMMM

**1 John 3:11 For this is the message which
you have heard from the beginning,
that we should love one another...**

MMMM... I'd like to think our children couldn't start their week without MMMM. I picture each of them getting ready for school or work and thinking, "What shall I do first. Make coffee, have a shower, or read MMMM?" Yes, I'm exaggerating a bit, but I do think the children love MMMM.

I'm going to keep you wondering about this one for a while, so don't sneak ahead of me.

MMMM began in 2006, at a time when the Lord was once again stretching me as a mother. I knew He was preparing me to let go of our son Jamison, who was in grade 12. After much prayer he decided that upon graduation he'd attend His Hill Bible School in Comfort, Texas, as his two older sisters had done. We were delighted, but it also meant I'd have to face yet another empty bedroom in our home. We already had two of them that were hard to walk by daily.

The prospect of three vacant rooms and only one child left at home by that September left me in a position to make some choices. I could...

A. Begin crying in despair, (but I think I'd done that a few times before and found it didn't help).
B. Throw myself at the only child left at home, (not a good idea).
C. Turn to the Lord for His sufficiency and grace, (just the thing we'd been talking to the children about for years).

Girls, this time I got it right. I chose option C. And the Lord began something new in my life.

As I looked to Him for sufficiency and grace, He blessed me with not only His peace, but also with a few creative thoughts. In His kindness, one Monday morning He gave me a *(gasp) I have an idea!* moment.

I went to the computer and created a group e-mail called Amazing Kids that was made up of our four children. From my fingertips came the letters MMMM on the subject line of the e-mail. It stood for Mom's Monday Morning Memo. God put me onto something that I couldn't explain, but I just typed without a plan.

MMMM is e-mailed to all the children no matter where they live, in the downstairs bedroom or 1,800 miles away. It's become a weekly institution. Contents? Whatever the Lord wants. Personal updates, family news, prayer requests for each other, upcoming events, passages of

Scripture, questionnaires, humorous stories, answers to prayer, silly stuff, numbing winter temperatures in Saskatchewan... whatever the Lord desires.

I estimate that I've sent out approximately 250 MMMM to our children. I usually send it out first thing Monday morning, while I linger over my coffee. It's a moment of thanksgiving I have before the Lord each week. I pray that it shows the children how much they are loved by Ron and me, as well as by the Lord. MMMM is only one small way to show them this, but it's a weekly reminder of His love for them through their family.

Here's a close up look at our family. Please enjoy MMMM from today, Monday, January 26, 2009.

Good morning all... welcome once again to MMMM... I know you all have been waiting for this... dad and I just finished chapter 12 of The Normal Christian Life by Watchman Nee... such a great chapter on the soul... if any of you have time to re-read this book, go for it... or even just that chapter... I encourage you Calgary kids to get any of your Bible school books out again, you will read them differently the second time... trust God to reveal Himself to you. (I know Genevieve and Brooklynne finished reading it.) Anyhow... I am home for most of the day... too cold to head out right now... -47°C... or something like that... but you can pray for me this afternoon... I am having coffee with a young grade 12 girl I know... the Lord has prompted me to visit with her and present her with the idea of His Hill in Sept. '09... tonight dad and I are having family and friends feast at the restaurant (see **side note** at the end of this chapter) with Ray and Lori Fournier... what could be nicer than time with fabulous friends like them on a cold winter night?

Pray for Genevieve... allergies

Pray for Brooklynne... spring break plans

Pray for Jamo... new job!

Pray for Alexandra... she's making her debut as a wedding planner for Janelle's wedding

Pray for dad... as he finishes year-end

Pray for me.... to warm up!

Hey, I have an idea... kind of outside the box... would anyone like to volunteer to do next Monday's MMMM?... you could even put your initial in place of the M for mom... that could be fun... you would not be stuck with the job each week... just for once?? Any offers? I will take the first offer I get... (in case I have a number of volunteers).... bless y'all today... love you... love mxoxmoxmoxmoxmoxmxmoxmoomxxmoxomxo xmoxom

Side note: We own and operate two seafood restaurants here in Regina. Well, they really belong to the Lord, we're just running them for Him.

Three

Free Tuition

**Numbers 6:24-26 The LORD bless you, and
keep you; The LORD make His face
shine on you,
And be gracious to you;
The LORD lift up His countenance on you,
And give you peace.**

I know a lot of weird things.

I know what a misty flip is, I know what an ollie is, I know what edge you take off on for a double loop, and I know what double bounce and double bow mean. I know what a half pipe is. I know what straight edge, heel edge and edgy mean. I know what wicked, sick and word mean. I know what looping means. And I know what CPRS and WOT stand for. I know what it means to drop in. I know what old school, ready go, and ready ok mean. I know what campused and points mean. I know what Klingbeils are. I know what it means to hit the rail. I know what the writing-in book is and what shoe-check means. I know what a

28

flight, Maytoberfest and a client are. I know what 'rents, timmy-hos and sbucks mean. I know what goofie and fixed gear mean. I know what a quiz meet is.

I know where Asessippi, Mission Ridge, Milky Way, 13th Ave. Coffee House, Krispy Kreme, Rudy's, Java South, Cozi, HEB, High's, Kicking Horse, Ross, Whole Foods, Anthropologie, Marble Slab, Bankers Hall, Angkor and Tommy Burger all are. I know where Dark Hall, Emmanuel, Grace House, Hobby Lobby, Nellies, Dutch Cycle, Long and McQuade and the Gospels are located.

I know when and why to cheer at hockey, lacrosse, figure skating, badminton, soccer, synchronized swimming, basketball and football events. I know about chamber choir, vocal jazz, senior choir, instrumental jazz, symphonic winds and wind ensemble concerts and Romanian dance recitals.

You get the point.

And over a period of time I began to get the point from God. I could see Him doing something very fulfilling in my life as a mother, as He unfolded His plan for our family. It was a beautiful treasure from heaven.

You see girls, I fell in love with Ron in 1978, but I've fallen in love a few times since then; when each of the children was born- November, 1983, in August, 1985, again in March, 1988 and one more time in October, 1990. Words can't describe how much I love our children. You know what I'm talking about.

But beyond that, I believe the Lord gave me His perfect idea to dedicate a portion of my life to their lives, and also their interests. He ignited a spark that blazed in me creating an eagerness to fulfill this calling for my life. What a gift it is as I live my life in Jesus Christ!

And what a joy it's been with the Lord as He's positioned me in our children's lives for the past 27 years. I've explored, explained, examined, exclaimed and experienced exhaustion. But it's also a treasure I'd never trade. I've listened, learned, laughed, looked and loved. I wouldn't have had it any other way. I've packed, planned, played, prayed and promised. I've smiled, stared, suggested and served.

By the grace of God alone, the children seemed to comprehend that it was the Lord's calling for me to devote a portion of my life to theirs. However, the Lord has taught me there are times to be actively involved and times to step back. And then there are the times I have to be reminded that He is Lord. He's Lord over them and I need to commit and submit to Him. I'm learning, I'm learning.

Here's something I've learned that came easily and has eternal rewards. It's learning about what your children are all about. The great thing about this education is that you don't even have to go back to school. The classroom is right in your own home.

No tuition, application deadlines, registration fee, personal profiles to fill out, no reference checks, portfolios, interviews, shortlists, competition, hidden costs, no waiting for the letter. Plus, it's never too late to become a student of your own child or the children in your life- grandchildren, nieces, nephews and family friends. May I suggest you ask the Lord to place some young people in your life in which you can take a godly interest? Eternal rewards.

So what does it look like to become a student of your child?

- Read your child's favourite book.
- Invite your child to bring their best-loved music to play in the car. Ask about the musician and about the genre of music. If you use the word genre, it will blow your child away!
- Inquire about their teachers. What do they like most about those people?
- Ask them to show you some of their "tricks"... on the monkey bars, skating rink and trampoline, or with their skateboard, snowboard, wakeboard, skipping rope, hockey stick and yo-yo.
- Ask them about their friends (be careful how you approach this one). Be sincere if you ask who they really like to hang around with and who their true friends are and why.
- Ask them if they'd like to have a few friends over for lunch, dinner, cookies, playtime, a movie, a sleepover or a tea party. Our little ones used to love tea parties and we've seen a lively interest in tea drinking resurface in our home during the teen and young adult years. Drinking unique teas has become a big hit and a popular reason for a gathering around the kitchen table (I've learned not to call them tea parties anymore).
- Tell them about the friends you had when you were 10, 16 and 21. And the choices you made.

- Go, go, go. Go to their games, practices, concerts, shows, performances, competitions, meets, school and field trips. Make time and go. Even if you can't make it to the whole event, try to catch the beginning or the end. Implement a "be there" policy in your life. And speak graciously when you connect with them afterwards.
- Make cookies for anything and everything you can. Or buy them. Just take cookies. Who doesn't enjoy a cookie?
- Get to know anyone who teaches or coaches your child anything. Take them cookies too.
- Have food around. Popcorn is simple, inexpensive and quick to prepare. You can easily feed an army of teens. Children can make it themselves and clean up is easy. Popcorn has saved me dozens of times and the aroma is so welcoming as hungry ones burst through the door. The smell of popcorn says, "You mean so much to me, I've been waiting for you all to come home and I've got a wonderful snack ready, have a seat and dig in." (And it only took you five minutes to make it.)
- Volunteer for events involving your child, even for a few hours. Talk about it when you get home. It's a great opportunity for a conversation starter.
- Invite your child to go on a date- lunch, coffee or dessert at their favourite place. Then next time take them to your favourite place. Get coffee and go for a walk.

- If they live away from home, plan a trip (with their blessing of course) to visit and explore their town.
- Learn to text message. Learn to say please, thank you and I'm sorry to your children.

You get the point again.

Here's an idea for you to consider. I believe that if you inquire of the Lord how to become a student of your child, He'll walk you right into a *(gasp) I have an idea!* moment and through a fabulous journey of your own. Along the way, keep praying a beautiful Old Testament blessing over those little ones in your care- Numbers 6:24-26. The LORD bless you, and keep you; The LORD make His face shine on you, and be gracious to you; The LORD lift up His countenance on you, and give you peace.

Popcorn with a Twist

1 great big bowl of freshly made hot popcorn
1/3 cup melted butter
2 t. curry powder (Yes, that's right, curry powder! We use mild.)
1/2 t. salt

Combine the butter with the curry powder and salt. Feel free to adjust the seasonings to suit your family's tastes. Toss the butter mixture into the hot popcorn and let your family and friends enjoy. Curried popcorn made its debut on the buffet table at our annual Christmas party about a decade ago and became an instant hit. It's made a joyous appearance every year since then. But it's just as good the rest of the year!

Four

Personal, Playful and Prayerful

Genesis 1:14 Then God said, "Let there be lights in the expanse of the heavens to separate the day from the night, and let them be for signs and for seasons and for days and years..."

Personal

When I sense the first signs of autumn, I announce that it's my favourite season. The morning of the first fluffy snowfall, I decide that winter is surely my favourite season. When spring finally buds, I smile, nod and say, spring is by far my favourite season, and when golf season, oops, I mean summer arrives, I declare this is truly my favourite season.

But to be totally honest, fall is my best-loved time of the year for many reasons. It's all about the fall fruits and vegetables, warm sweaters, back to school excitement, homey décor, hearty soups and walks through the leaves in cool air. It's a time of year for the Lord to show off His unmatched creativity with colour and His handiwork in dynamically sketched skies.

It also means three autumn-only activities around our home. Here's a personal one, playful one and prayerful one.

Let's get Personal

There's a buzz in the air at the beginning of each September that makes me sad. It's the sound of so many mothers rejoicing that their children are out of their hair and back to school. Call me weird, but I admit I loved having our children and their friends around all summer. In and out, slamming doors, wet feet running through the house and damp towels on the floor. In my mind, those were signs of a great summer. Back-to-school always meant no more beach days, holiday times, lazy mornings, pool parties, ice cream runs or lemonade stands.

Back-to-school eve always made me pout. Come to think of it, it still does. But now rather than seeing our children walk two short blocks down the street to school, we have emotional and soggy goodbyes at airports as they go thousands of miles away to college. But that's another whole chapter.

I've said it time and time again. God is good and greatly to be praised. Oh, how He can turn our sorrow into joy. I suppose if I'd not had those teary back-to-school times, this particular story wouldn't have been written.

One waterlogged back-to-school eve, I received the gift of a *(gasp) I have an idea!* moment from the Lord. After the children had all been tucked into bed, I found a quiet place in our home and began to write a letter to each of them. I wasn't really sure what I was going to write, but the Lord said write, and so I did.

What evolved were four very personal hand written (remember those?) letters, one to each child that was a tender reflection of the past year, and a prayerful look at the coming year. These letters of thanksgiving to God took some uninterrupted time to compose and required a drying period before I could seal them up. I discovered that tears cause ink to run a bit. Each letter was dated, enveloped, sealed, and safely deposited in a drawer I'd set aside for such special treasures.

Each year, on back-to-school eve, I'd conduct this rather sentimental ritual and tuck away the letters after an intimate time with the Lord. I had no clear plan in mind when to give these to the children, but I trusted God to show me His purpose. And then one day it happened. I was completing a scrapbook for Genevieve for her high school graduation and I got an idea!

I went to the drawer and pulled out the envelope with her name on it. In it were 13 little envelopes dated back to 1988. I slipped them into the last page of her high school scrapbook and smiled with thanksgiving at the Lord. Upon graduation she received this book of praise to God for the life He'd given her for 18 years. I prayed it would be a special time for her and the Lord as she sat down with Him to quietly read all the heartfelt letters He'd prompted me to write her over the years.

I've happily handed out scrapbooks and fat envelopes of letters to all the children as they finished high school. I don't write anymore back-to-school letters, but I'm sort of thinking that when we have grandchildren... well, I'd better not run ahead of the Lord.

Now let's get Playful

On windy autumn days I often stand at my kitchen window watching the beauty of the Lord as golden leaves pour off the trees in our backyard. In southern Ontario where I was raised the leaves are brilliant crimson, burnt orange and precious gold. One of the first assignments elementary school children in the Niagara Peninsula have each September is a leaf project. School children on the prairies don't seem to get that assignment. Imagine that. So one luscious autumn day I got an idea and took it upon myself to do a leaf project with our children here at home.

A few days later I set to work preparing the materials for our project and by the time they burst in the door at 3:30 I was vibrating with excitement over this new craft idea. "Leaf placemats!" I exclaimed with an eager smile. They downed a quick snack and dove into this new fall activity with the utmost enthusiasm. We have great children.

Ladies, this craft is simple and good for children of any age. Just head outdoors for most of your materials- no need to run from store to store looking for obscure supplies. Look to God's creation and revel in Him as you search for the prettiest leaves and unique twigs with your children.

Press the leaves between sheets of wax paper in the pages of a heavy book. When craft day arrives, glue your finds to autumn coloured construction paper in a size to suit your table, add a few stickers and cover the placemat with clear sticky paper. Voilà! You have a functional craft your children can use three times a day for at least a few months. The children have even made placemats for Ron and me.

We've done this craft for many years. Fall wouldn't be fall without a spread of leaf placemats. Even as teenagers, they were thrilled to come home from a long day at school and see the makings of leaf placemats on the table. Especially for teens, this proved to be a relaxing time for them after school, before retreating to their rooms for hours of homework. As our children headed off to college, the "at-home" children would make personalized leaf placemats and send them to their siblings. I often wondered what college roommates thought when these crafts arrived in the mail.

A few years ago after a leaf placemat making session, our son Jamison who was about 19 years old at the time, announced, "Mom this will probably make you cry, but I want you to know something. I will definitely be making leaf placemats with my children some day." Then he stood there with a smile waiting for my response. I melted into the closest chair as he enjoyed a tender little chuckle. I really do love being a mother.

And now let's be Prayerful

Have you ever noticed the adorable ornamental mini pumpkins that appear in the floral department of the grocery store in the early fall? If not, you simply must look for them next September. They're one of the cutest little things I've ever seen. I know it's a sure sign of autumn when I encounter these chubby little gourds as I'm picking out root vegetables for a fall stew.

I don't think I'm being overly dramatic when I say that it was a special moment in my life the morning I discovered these mini treasures many years ago. Have I mentioned how much I love the fall? Have I mentioned how much I love Jesus? Sorry, that was a little tangent.

As soon as I met these precious little pumpkins I knew I had to add one to my fall home décor. No, I needed more than one. Girlfriend, they're only a dollar. I bought a few. By the time I got them home, I had another one of God's great big beautiful ideas brewing in my head. (**Warning:** one must exercise extreme caution when driving and contemplating big ideas.)

I couldn't wait to proudly display my new decorations on the kitchen table, and see a response from my beloved family. To my surprise and joy a little voice from the crowd asked if she could decorate a pumpkin. Before I knew it I was back at the store to purchase one for each member of the family. It wasn't long until we had the fabric paint and nail polish out to embellish the pumpkins. Each child delighted in displaying their artistry in the center of the table. This has become another relished activity each fall in our home. Life is good.

Our six little pumpkins are a daily reminder to me to pray for our family. I spend much of my day in and around the kitchen, otherwise known as command central. And as I catch glimpses of these irresistible little ornaments, I praise God for His life in each member of our family.

One autumn a few years ago Ron and I became what some people call empty nesters. (That's a term I dislike so much I dedicated a whole chapter to it. Hint: Chapter 32... Freedom 51.) So, at the first sign of fall, I went to the grocery store and purchased six of the most darling pumpkins. I arranged them lovingly on the kitchen table as a reminder to lift our children up to the Lord daily in prayer with thanksgiving.

I've also discovered baby pumpkins travel quite well through the mail system. I love not only having the gourds as part of our fall décor, but it's also a playful idea to send far off children a piece of their childhood that says they're loved and in our prayers daily. I love God's ideas.

How can I possibly end this autumn chapter without a couple of good pumpkin recipes? Here are two unique ones we love.

Pump-me-up Pumpkin Coffee

1 T. canned pumpkin
1/2 cup milk
1 t. vanilla
1 t. brown sugar or a splash of pumpkin syrup

1/2 t. cinnamon
1 cup hot coffee

Heat the pumpkin and milk in a small saucepan. Add the vanilla and sugar. Whisk well to blend all ingredients. Pour the coffee into your prettiest fall mug and top with the pumpkin mixture. Stir and sprinkle with cinnamon. Ahh....

And I think you're going to love this one... it makes me smile.

Pumpkin goes for a Dip

8 oz. cream cheese, softened
1 cup brown sugar
2 cups canned pumpkin
1 T. cinnamon
1 T. pumpkin pie spice
1 t. nutmeg
1 t. vanilla
1 T. frozen orange juice concentrate, thawed

Are you ready for this culinary surround sound of flavour? Combine all the ingredients together and blend them until they're nice and smooth. It's that easy. I'm picturing this dip served in a rustic pottery bowl or wide mouthed canning jar. Chill it for 8 hours or overnight. You can serve this as an appetizer or dessert with ginger snaps, graham crackers, apple wedges and pear slices. So good, so different, so easy.

Five

Gold, Frankincense and Myrrh

Matthew 2:11 After coming into the house they saw the Child with Mary His mother; and they fell to the ground and worshiped Him. Then, opening their treasures, they presented to Him gifts of gold, frankincense and myrrh.

Gold

Gold- [gould] noun- a highly precious metal used as currency, in jewelry, art, and for ornamentation or embellishment.

It was the mid 1980s. I was a young mom at home with a four-year-old, two-year-old and I was six months pregnant. We'd been living in Red Deer, Alberta for less than a year, but I could already see how God had gone before us and prepared the hearts of a lovely group of women who befriended me.

During this wonderful time in my life the Lord picked up His royal pen and began to write what appeared to be a simple little story. But by the final chapter, His idea had unfolded into what has become a key element in our family's Christmas traditions.

Here's how this glorious idea came to pass. One morning a sweet new friend suggested a group of us have a craft morning. We all quickly ran for our glue guns and glitter. Then she suggested we make Christmas activity calendars. We all quickly ran for our construction paper and crayons. Not so quickly, I thought to myself. Forget the construction paper and crayons, even if they were sparkly. I had a better idea.

I'd recently learned to quilt. (When I think back on it, how in the world did I have the time or energy to quilt? Hand quilt! Oh well.) I began to think about quilting an Advent activity calendar to hang in our home. It was already mid-November, which only gave me a few weeks to complete it for December 1st. Hmm... what was I thinking? It must've been the second trimester hormones acting up. But when the Lord sets my mind to something He initiates, I become a woman on a mission. Does anybody agree with me?

There was a charming, local quilting store I frequented that had the perfect fabrics I needed- rich green velvet, deep crimson and a gold Christmas print. As the children napped, I cut fabric. As they played, I created patterns. As they coloured, I quilted. On December 1st, with Christmas music swirling in our home, the Advent activity calendar made its historic debut. Twenty-four little plastic rings that I'd carefully sprayed gold to match the fabric hung on our strip quilted wall hanging. Each ring held a rolled piece of glittering paper with a special Christmas activity written on it for every day leading up to Christmas.

I was delighted with the finished project. Interestingly though, what I thought was a completed assignment, was really the start of a new tradition that would continue each December for decades. This year marked the 23rd year of the Advent calendar.

We had wonderful times together daily-colouring Christmas pictures, baking cookies, decorating, playing in the snow, attending concerts and everything Christmassy you could imagine. I was in my glory and the children could barely wait to discover what the hidden activity was in the tiny scroll each day. Although all of this had originally started as simply an activity calendar, we began to sense the Lord had a more meaningful purpose to add to this December celebration.

He gave me another idea. I began to add a prayer request to each small paper. Prayers for family, missionaries, pastors, the homeless and so many more. Now we not only had a special little something to do daily, we also had a little prayer time as a family. Even as the children got older, the activities were always fun, but God showed us the difference between a playful time and a prayerful time. The tiny gold rings on the quilt held memory building moments like chopping down the Christmas tree, but more importantly, inside those golden rings were prayers waiting to be released into heaven's throne room.

We've all heard the expression, "She's got a heart of gold." Girls, let's not hang onto those hearts of gold. Instead let's be willing to hand our hearts over to the Lord in worship through prayer. And remember, silence is golden, especially before the Lord.

For those of you who want details...

Our quilted tree is a simple triangular Christmas tree shape, made up of two-inch wide strips of fabric, quilted together and has a brown corduroy tree trunk. I did some quick calculations. Over 23 years we've enjoyed an estimated 552 activities and prayers. Some of the many activities...

Making snow forts, Christmas shopping, reading Christmas books, card-making, baking, decorating, gingerbread house and cookie making, caroling, ice skating, tobogganing, tree chopping, attending Christmas concerts, making food hampers, serving at the Christmas dessert theatre outreach at our church, shoveling snow (look at how creative I can be!), attending a Christmas musical production at a nearby Bible college, planning a family Christmas party, building snowmen, helping with the family Christmas cards (more creative planning), dressing in red and green and having special Christmas play days with friends, getting Christmas books from the library...

Prayers have included: family members near and far, travelers, students finishing their semester, pastors, pastor's families, Christmas outreach programs, neighbours, missionaries, shut-ins, homeless, people who receive our Christmas card, grieving friends, the new year, thanks for the past year, our church family, and focusing on Christ through all the tinsel.

Frankincense

Frankincense- [frang-kin-sens] noun- aromatic gum resin from Asian and African trees. Frankincense is used in incense and perfumes; we also know it as one of the three gifts the magi brought to Jesus.

The fragrance of freshly baked shortbread cookies says the holidays are in the air. A roasting turkey smells just like Christmas and freshly baked gingerbread is a classic holiday aroma. But what is it about the glorious scent of a freshly cut Christmas tree that surpasses every one of these bouquets? You can't beat the homey, piney and comforting fragrance of a freshly cut tree that's nestled its way into a family room. The fresh tree makes itself at home quickly, and instantly becomes the family's gathering point at Christmas. For two weeks in December, the most coveted spot in the family room is the cozy chair closest to the tree.

We've always had a fresh Christmas tree in our family room. An attractive, artificial tree stands in the living room, but it smells like... nothing. It's pretty and stylish, very co-coordinated and chic, but that's about it. We all prefer to gather around the fresh tree. We've done so for 33 Christmases.

Trees of every size and shape have burst through the front doors of our home. Some of the trees we've welcomed have brought smiles and cheers; some have simply brought on the tears. Others seemed to have quadrupled in size once exposed to the warmth of a loving home. And still others appeared to have shed all their dignity during the drive home from the tree lot.

Some things never change and this includes the day we get our tree. With frozen fingers and frostbitten toes, Ron meticulously cares for his investment. Once the prized possession arrives in our garage, he ceremoniously cuts a few inches off the trunk in order to open up the pores, which have been clogged with sap. (This cut will allow the tree to drink the water in which it proudly stands for several weeks.)

One cold December night many years ago I lovingly watched Ron shiver as he performed this annual tree surgery in the garage. Then it happened. Just as he was about to toss the two-inch stub of trunk in the garbage I gasped and got an idea. He couldn't possibly throw out that little stump. I quickly snatched it up and dashed into the house. With a permanent marker, I inscribed the year 1992 onto the freshly cut stump. I placed it on the hearth and thus began an annual tradition. We now have 18 different stumps in our collection, each one unique and dated.

The first few years this ritual just seemed like a nice idea. But as the stump forest grew, a couple of interesting things became apparent. We could see a symbol of many blessed years together as a family. As well, the collection of stumps has caused us to reminisce about the precious Christmases God has given us. Have I mentioned that God has great ideas?

Without fail, each year when the children see this collection, they comment on all the trees of the past and the growing number of stumps. Someone in the family always makes sure we haven't forgotten to add the latest stub to the growing portfolio. I truly believe it's those simple little gifts from the Lord that influence the children so much more than costly luxuries.

I always set the stump forest up on one corner of the hearth, along with a basket of pinecones and evergreen bows. When friends offer to stoke the fire, we quickly instruct them that the precious stumps aren't firewood. Can you imagine if...?

Aromas. Hmm... Scripture talks about an aroma that's soothing or pleasing to the Lord. Would you ask yourself what type of aroma rises from your life up to the heavenlies? Is it one that pleases and soothes the Lord God Almighty? I'll let you and the Lord discuss that while I slip into the kitchen and whip up a little batch of shortbread.

Myrrh

Myrrh- [mur] noun- a reddish-brown resinous material, the dried sap from trees in Yemen and Somalia; another one of the gifts the magi brought to Jesus.

A gift- something voluntarily bestowed without payment in return, showing favour toward someone to honour an occasion.

And don't some of us seem to take that to the extreme at Christmas? I love gift giving. I also delight in celebrating Jesus not only at Christmas, but year 'round. So when I combine two things I love, Jesus and gift giving, wonderful things happen. One Christmas the Lord gave me a unique gift giving idea with a kingdom twist.

Although God had seen all the hoopla over gift giving in our lives, I believe He prompted me to add one more special item to my gift list, for His glory and for His pleasure.

Our three children were still little- two, five and seven years old (it doesn't matter how old Ron and I were, I'll just tell you we were young enough to still have some fun). Christmas day was coming to a leisurely close by the fire. We were all content, basking in God's rich blessings as a family, doing what is biblical- dining and reclining. You know the kind of Christmas night I'm talking about.

Suddenly I sat up awkwardly straight in my cozy chair, wide-eyed as I scanned the room and gasped. Recognizing that very familiar sound and sight, my family looked at me suspiciously. I had an idea!

Although there were no more presents under the twinkling lights of the tree, God was asking us to give out one more gift of thanksgiving for the One who is the Light of the world. We were about to embark on the best gift-giving extravaganza we'd ever experience. No list to make, no internet to surf, no stores to rummage through, no wrapping to be done, no size to guess, no colour to decide and no price to be paid. It was a gift for the One who paid the price for us.

Picture this. After the initial gasp, I proposed that we should act out the Christmas story together. Each person would choose a character from the Christmas story in the books of Matthew or Luke. The angel of the Lord would read Luke 2:1-20 aloud. I could sense everyone's enthusiasm as we scurried around the house to find costumes and props. There was freedom to go into any room or closet to find whatever was needed.

Twenty-two pageants later, the same rules still apply. No planning ahead of time for roles or accessories. Everything all comes together in five minutes and then the curtain rises. It was our simple gift of thanks to the Lord, but the simplicity didn't in any way minimize its significance in our hearts. This was to be an act of worship, our myrrh to Him.

We always have a Mary and Joseph, some shepherds, a few kings and the angel of the Lord. That very first pageant in 1989 was so memorable. As you can imagine, the photo is hilarious. My parents were Mary and Joseph, Genevieve and I were the shepherds, Ron and one-year-old Jamison were kings and Alexandra was the angel. There was an assortment of stuffed animals as well as my parent's dog. Sadly, baby Jesus is unidentifiable in the picture. I'd venture to say a doll of some sort. In 1990, when Brooklynne was only three-months-old, she was our baby Jesus, swaddled angelically in a makeshift manger.

I want to share with you the irony of the photo of the 1989 pageant. Each year after we are finished our little production, we carefully set the automatic timer on the camera to capture a precious picture of the cast. But in that very first photo, centered in the background of the shot, is a huge (tacky) crocheted wall hanging of Santa's head! The Saviour and Santa in the same picture. I'm happy to say that Jesus is alive and living in our home 22 years later. The crocheted, nylon Santa head was retired years ago.

The children have described the Annual Gladysz Family Christmas Pageant as a must-do part of Christmas. We must give thanks to the Lord for his gift of Jesus to us. We do have great fun for a few minutes gathering fur and feathers, tiaras and towels, bathrobes and babies for the pageant. But when the angel of the Lord begins to read the Word of God, there's a reverence that settles upon all of us. We listen to the Word recognizing that He is the center of our lives.

The whole thing only takes about ten minutes. But they're the most precious moments of our entire Christmas season. God has great ideas and I am humbled that He chose to pass this one on to me. I gasp in awe of Him.

Our friends have heard we do this each year. Many have asked us who watches our pageant. I think they assume there are some guests who enjoy the pageant with us. We're tempted to admit there's no audience at all. But then we correct ourselves. It's for the Lord, of course! An audience of One. The One whom it's all about. So year after year, we continue to present Him with this Christmas gift... our myrrh to Him!

We couldn't wait for the year we had a new addition to the family. Finally there was Chris, the new son-in-law! There had been many conflicting ideas regarding which part should be assigned to the newest member of the family. Chris made his debut as Joseph.

One of the most famous and fabulous Christmas aromas is the fragrance of freshly baked shortbread. I see you nodding. Everyone has a favourite recipe for this cookie. So I won't tell you this one is the greatest thing that will ever happen to your lips or hips. I'll just say that our family loves it, and I've been making it for decades. It's our Christmas love language. I call it...

Walking in a Winter Wonderland Whipped Shortbread

1 cup butter (no margarine please!)
1/2 cup icing sugar
1 1/2 cups all purpose flour

Cream the butter and sugar well. I use my mixer with the paddle attachment, but you can even use a hand mixer. Switch to the whipping attachment and gradually add the flour. Then beat for about 8-10 minutes. Yes, that long. The batter will be fluffy and white, like a beautiful mound of snow. Drop a heaping tablespoon of dough onto a cookie sheet leaving each cookie piled up like a snowdrift. Your baking sheet will look like a walk through a winter wonderland. Hum to yourself. Decorate each cookie with crushed candy canes, red sprinkles or the traditional maraschino cherry. It's Christmas, so I break down and eat half of a maraschino cherry.

Bake these at 350° F. for about 10-12 minutes, until they barely begin to brown. This recipe will make about 30 cookies, but I always double it. Don't fool yourself. You can very possibly eat a couple dozen straight out of the oven. Store them in tins, in a good hiding place.

Ahh... the fragrance! Ohh... sleigh bells ring, are you listening?

Six

T.O.T.M.C.

**2 Corinthians 9:7 Each one must do just as
he has purposed in his heart, not grudgingly
or under compulsion, for God loves
a cheerful giver.**

I struggle with putting a plain, white envelope
into the mailbox.

A delightful British woman works at our neighbourhood post office. She tells my husband that
she looks forward to the carefully embellished
packages and envelopes that he's faithfully taken
there weekly for a decade. There's probably no
need to tell you that it's not Ron who decorates
these items bound for Texas or western Canada.
I admit I have issues. I simply can't put a naked
envelope into the mail system. One sticker, even
one sticker makes all the difference.

Stickers, photos, magazine or newspaper clip-
pings all work for me. A little clear packing tape
seals things up and the happy package is good to
go. On his way to work my sweet husband does

a weekly post office run for me with these pieces of art.

But the real fun begins before I get to the packaging stage. It's what's inside that matters. Kind of like our hearts. When the Lord gives me an idea for how He wants to bless the children through a surprise package, I become His cheerful giver. And at the beginning of 2008, the Lord treated me to a *(gasp) I have an idea!* moment.

T.O.T.M.C. Treat of the Month Club. It excites me to even write about it. The Treat of the Month Club was for the two "away" girls. Genevieve was in ministry in Texas and Alexandra was in her last year of college in Calgary. So monthly, each girl would receive a package in the mail throughout the year.

Genevieve's treat was called Sweater of the Month Club. She'd receive a shirt, top or sweater of some sort. Brooklynne worked at a funky little clothing store and always found the most darling items on sale for me to send. Genevieve loved this idea and looked forward to a monthly addition to her wardrobe. I delighted in looking through good sale racks for the right sweater for her, then decorating the package with a Tex-Mex theme. The Lord was faithful to always show me the perfect treat for her at a very reasonable price each month.

Alexandra's monthly surprise was Gift Card of the Month Club. I was tickled pink each month to send her a fancied-up envelope with a special gift card in it. Coffee shop, grocery store, drug store or bake shop. As a student, she admitted every little bit helped.

Girls, with a flick of a sticker, I was overjoyed to hand these treasures to Ron as he headed off to work, via the post office. This year things look a bit different. Genevieve now receives A.O.T.M.C. Translation: Accessory of the Month Club. I hunt out great bargains on adorable bracelets, unusual earrings, stylish necklaces, fun scarves and big rings. And how I praise God for always directing me to a good sale.

God says in His Word that He loves a cheerful giver. How good it is to give. How much better it is to give cheerfully, as we give from what He's given to us.

While we're on the topic of packages for those "away" children in your life, here are a few ideas of items I've sent over the years.

Newspaper articles, recipes, baby pictures, old humorous photos, church bulletins, pepperoni sticks, Bible verses on pretty paper, love notes, air fresheners (whose dorm room doesn't need an air freshener?), snacks like potato chips, ginger snaps (they travel well), healthy crackers, granola bars, gum, jump drives, razor blades (you may know a college man who needs to be reminded to shave occasionally), and even a picture of Ron and me. One year I asked Genevieve's friends for hand written notes and sent a puffy envelope stuffed with special thoughts to her for her birthday.

I've had a lot of fun sending the children a game of unscramble-the-letters. I cut pieces of paper into one-inch squares and on each square I wrote a letter that formed a word when laid out in the proper order. I scrambled the little papers and put them in an envelope (that's been decorated!). I included instructions on the envelope (or they would've really wondered about me and this envelope of random letters). I usually sent this game shortly before Christmas break, when thoughts of coming home were beginning to swirl in their minds. I used words such as Christmas oranges, whipped shortbread and candy cane bark. Things they fondly associated with Christmas at home.

Because I really like you, I'd like to share this sweetie with you. Check out the variations, be creative. It's a little something from my kitchen to yours. Let me know how you like it. Let's become foodies together.

Candy Cane Bark with a Bite

2 cups good quality white chocolate pieces
1/2 cup crushed candy canes- to crush these use the pulse button on your food processor or place candy canes in a heavy-duty sealable plastic bag and smash it with a rolling pin into the desired size. Smashing is fun.

Wait patiently for the first snowfall, and then put on some Christmas music.

Head to the kitchen and cover a cookie sheet with waxed paper or parchment paper. Melt the chocolate in a double boiler or in a bowl over a pot of boiling water (be careful because chocolate burns easily). Blend the crushed candy canes into the melted chocolate, pour this onto your cookie sheet and using a spatula to spread it evenly. I like a thickness of between 1/8th and 1/4 inch. Refrigerate the bark for at least 15 minutes. When it has hardened, break it into pieces and store it in tins or airtight containers. Hide these treats well. The bark will last for a month, if no one finds it.

There are variations galore. Omit the candy canes and use any combination of chopped dried apricots, dried cranberries, pumpkin seeds, pistachios, cashew pieces or dried cherries. Pecans are good too. Very good. If dark or milk chocolate makes your toes curl, then use those. This is an absolutely scrumptious addition to Christmas. Great for gift giving. Mmm....

Seven

The Rest Doesn't Really Matter

1 Peter 3:15 ... but sanctify Christ as Lord in your hearts, always being ready to make a defense to everyone who asks you to give an account for the hope that is in you, yet with gentleness and reverence...

I think that one of the most commonly asked questions during the Christmas season is, "So, are you ready for Christmas?"

Rarely do I ever hear anyone actually say; "I sure am," with any enthusiasm. As I pondered this question, the Lord put a longing in my heart to provide a meaningful answer to this query. An answer that would point people to Christ, not to their to-do lists.

On any given day in December, you can find me in the grocery store. And so it was on this particular frosty morning. I'm sure I was humming "Let it Snow" to myself. Shoppers shopped, cashiers cashed and poinsettias pointed. Then it happened. The question of the season. I knew it was coming because the clerk had that quizzical look on her face. The question of the season was coming at me... "more rapid than eagles." I knew I wasn't prepared, as I'd so desperately wanted to be. Ahh... I thought. I've failed Him again. But God turned my focus off my inadequacies and towards Himself. He gently showed me that He'll never let me down. I just need to hear and obey.

"Soooooooo, are you ready for Christmas, Stephanie?" (I'm in the grocery store so often, I'm on a first-name basis with some of the cashiers.) I opened my mouth and to my astonishment something of divine value poured out.

"My heart is ready and the rest doesn't really matter," I blurted out.

I gasped. What? Where did that come from? Did I say that? Who said that?

The poor cashier stopped and stared at me. I felt as though the Christmas carols floating through the store came to a halt and everyone at the check-out was staring at me. I'm sure the lady behind me headed straight to the chiropractor because she jerked her head out of her cart so abruptly she needed an adjustment. Then the clerk smiled and responded something like, "Yeah, you're right. That's true."

In an instant, the Lord showed me once again that when Stephanie gets out of the way, there's so much room for God to do His perfect work. What a gift that moment was.

I walked away with a cartful of goodies and a heart full of gratitude to God. Grateful that in my inadequacy He's the great I AM, anywhere, anytime. And now even in June, I look forward to the Christmas season when I can smile and say... "My heart is ready and the rest doesn't really matter."

Eight

Gingerbread Houses and Graduation Gowns

Luke 1:50 AND HIS MERCY IS UPON GENERATION AFTER GENERATION TOWARD THOSE WHO FEAR HIM.

O nce upon a time there was a gingerbread house.

(At this point I want to add that I've often wondered if my heart beats to the rhythm of Jingle Bells in the month of December. I come from a long line of women who are over-the-top about Christmas.)

Ron and I were newlyweds celebrating our second Christmas together in our apartment with gecko green shag carpet and burnt orange accents. It was 1979. Did I even need to tell you that? That year I pined over the lack of Christmas décor in our little home, until I got the idea of a gingerbread house. It was as easy as mincemeat pie to convince a girlfriend to join me in this holiday fun. We had no idea what we were doing, but that didn't matter in the least to us.

As baking day drew closer I found myself gasping with delight at the thought of an adorable little Christmas cottage made out of gingerbread. I dreamt of something whimsical and inviting. I imagined creating a winter wonderland out of flour and sugar and candy.

After two full weekends, countless hours on our feet, gallons of royal decorator frosting, hundreds of pounds of candy and dozens of gingerbread pieces we proudly displayed our dazzling creations to our husbands. Ron was pretty impressed, until I told him he couldn't dream of eating anything off the house.

Our smiles shone brighter than silver bells as Ron and I posed for a quick picture beside our charming gingerbread house. Alas, that photo became our very first Christmas card picture. Happy newly-weds and a happy little house. We sent over 60 cards to family and friends that year. Ron with his 70's mustache, me and my waist-length, parted down the middle hair. Little did we know that as we snapped that picture, we were creating a family tradition that would become etched in stone like the Ten Commandments.

The Lord has blessed us each year by providing opportunities to capture a photo to use at Christmas. We have a classic snapshot in Banff on a bridge, and another chopping down our Christmas tree in the forest just outside Calgary. In 1983 we added a new family member. Wobbly-headed Genevieve was nine-days-old when we took that treasured shot. Two years later, Alexandra Joy showed up in the picture. A few years after that Jamison Troy joined our team and finally in 1990, Brooklynne completed our family. Our friends would write us saying that every few years it seemed as though we moved and added another baby to the picture. It was sort of true.

We now have a priceless collection of three decades of Christmas card pictures. Throughout the year, I'm always on the lookout for the right time to obtain the picture, especially these days when we're spread across North America and the six of us are not often together at the same time.

As the children have gotten older you can imagine that choosing the best picture has gotten trickier. Hmm... imagine that. There's often someone who's not happy with his or her hair (That was me this year; I had bad bangs in the picture because of the wind in Colorado.) Someone's always looking awkward or angry. Or we look too posed, or too casual. But the Lord always works it out. I know you can relate.

As I take a look back at these pictures I see us at Calaway Park, by our backyard pool and on a mountaintop near Lake Placid, New York. I see us all dressed in black and white (my weird idea of a theme), and I see the children all in Mickey Mouse attire. (We weren't even in Disneyland, but that was as close as we could get.) Then I see us cherry picking in Penticton, British Columbia. But what was I thinking one year when I included Miss Canada, who was speaking at our church, in the picture? Another year we used a picture of the six of us at Alexandra's high school graduation. The forest photo in Clear Lake, Manitoba became a favourite and a breath-taking river in Estes Park, Colorado was the backdrop for the 2008 picture.

This year's picture was monumental. After 22 years of the six-person photo, we added a new man! Chris, our first son-in-law. We're looking forward to the day the Lord grows our numbers with two more noble, young men and one special, godly woman.

Girlfriends, look at what our God is into. The Lord has placed the desire in our hearts to capture a family picture. Then He's cared enough to pen a specific time and occasion for us to gather for our treasured photo and some memory making. Each year in early December I bundle up and stroll down the street to the mailbox with an armful of Christmas cards. Before I pop them into the mail, I pray that the photo and letter will point our family and friends to Christ. We want our Christmas card pictures to be a way of exalting the Lord, "For the Mighty One has done great things for me; and holy is His name." Luke 1:49.

I'd like to make a suggestion. Please take a few minutes and read all of The Magnificat, Luke 1:46-55. Just read it. God will show you why.

Graduation Gowns

I'm so excited to write this chapter for you that my fingers can't possibly type as quickly as my thoughts are coming to me. I pray that God will bless you through these playful ideas as He's lavishly blessed our family. And once again, I want to encourage you to make them into what God intends for you and your loved ones.

Leaving these special Christmas photos in an envelope or box didn't seem right. I had no specific plans for what to do with them, but God sure did. One day when I was visiting my friend Carol, a director with Creative Memories, she showed me some of her new products. Stickers, paper, scrapbooking tools and a Christmas photo album. But it was that small red album that stole my heart and I purchased five of them before I left her home. God had given me an idea! As I headed home, ideas were unfolding in my head. Promise me you'll use the utmost caution if you are behind the wheel of your car when you're contemplating great ideas from the Lord.

By the time I arrived home I had it all planned out. Since I'd purchased five albums, there'd be an album for our home, and one for each of the children in which to mount years of family Christmas card photos. I pictured us having craft time... there'd be stickers, paper and every kind of supply needed to create stunning pages. I imagined us all around the kitchen table with our albums, eggnog and cookies; Christmas carols playing in the background. Can you picture it? Oh my, no pun intended. The children would become photo historians as they gathered around the table, eager to preserve the past. Oh glorious day!

In order to bring them all together for these kinds of events I have to plan wisely. Remember the Advent activity calendar from Chapter 5? That was the perfect avenue I needed to stage this new event. Tucked into one of the golden rings on that special craft day was a little scroll of paper which simply said, "Craft Time 3:00 p.m. at the kitchen table, everyone invited."

Let me remind you this big event occurred when all four of the children were teenagers. Even in their teen years our children loved crafts. They were raised on Jesus... and crafts.

When album making day finally arrived, I was shaking with excitement over this new idea. I spread out four albums on the table, along with Christmas stickers, paper, markers and 20 years of family Christmas card pictures. The children had all they needed to decorate their own keepsake album.

They know me well and could clearly see where I was going with this. They became artists, historians and journalists all in an hour. Each of the finished products was similar and yet different. It was an opportunity for each child to be creative and to have a tangible reminder of how God's face has shone upon us as a family.

Every year before Christmas the children know that one of the gold rings on the activity calendar will hold the announcement for album making. They come to the big old oak table with their photo album, ready to add that year's photo and to journal some memories.

I love how God uses these books, which can be passed on from one generation to another, to tell a family story of His blessings. God speaks to us through His Word, through the Holy Spirit and through other people. But He also uses our daily circumstances to communicate with us. It's interesting how God takes an ordinary thing like a photograph and turns it into a reminder of His great love for us, generation after generation.

At about the same time I began the Christmas albums, I had what I thought was a simple idea to make a scrapbook of Genevieve's life, as a high school graduation gift. That was the good news. The problem was that I was rather naive about the fine art of scrapbooking. It never really crossed my mind that this project could quickly grow out of control. Since she was the first child, I had thousands of pictures tucked away in boxes here and there. Are you nodding? It was a gigantic task, sorting, organizing and creating several scrapbooks in the end, but by the grace of God, they were completed in six months.

Needless to say, and I think you moms will agree with me, what you do with such magnitude for one child, you must do for all the rest. But on a smaller scale. As soon as I'd completed Genevieve's book, I began to work on Alexandra's graduation gift and then that project ran into Jamison's graduation. I had the system well organized by the time Brooklynne finished high school last spring.

It was a ton of work, but I cherished every moment of it. I may even go so far as to say that God graciously used scrapbooking to help me transition from mothering "at-home" children to nurturing "away" young adult children.

From gingerbread houses to graduation gowns and beyond, please keep your camera handy, have fresh batteries available and take pictures of your children. You'll never regret it. Your pictures could become a good record of God's mercy upon generation after generation.

Nine

Holiday or... Holy Day?

**Luke 2:14 "Glory to God in the highest,
And on earth peace among men
with whom He is pleased."**

I'm somewhat embarrassed to write this, but it has to be done. I have a confession to make and I'll get right to the point. I've written many obnoxious Christmas letters for many years, which I sent to many people.

Well, if that was supposed to make me feel better, I don't think it has, but I realize life is not all about how I feel. Perhaps by the end of this chapter I'll be more satisfied with my confession.

Good journalists always try to answer the questions, "what, why, who, where, when and how." So each year, in late fall, I'd try to produce what I thought was the "perfect" Christmas letter remembering these basic rules I learned at journalism school. Here's my different take on those rules.

- What: A Christmas letter, on the cutest holiday paper I could find, filled from top to bottom with information.
- Why: Because I was convinced every reader was dying to read what I had to write and needed to have this information in order for them to have a merry Christmas.
- Who: It went to many good friends and family.
- Where: The letter was lovingly folded, tucked into the card and sent all over the world.
- When: Mailed by early December.
- How: (Here comes the killer.) Honestly friends, it certainly wasn't under the inspiration of the Holy Spirit.

Each year in October I'd have a wonderful idea moment from the Lord. But then I'd proceed to ruin it with my pride, by producing what I thought was a fabulously creative letter for Christmas.

In order to properly pen this chapter I've made myself a cup of tea and worked my way through a file of past Christmas letters. Oh mercy me. After a long read, I realize I have a lot of apologizing to do. I certainly never intended to harass our family and friends, the people who I love so much, with my over the top Christmas letter.

You need to get a real look at what I'm talking about and since I (thankfully) can't show you the whole folder of letters, I'll give you a sample. Here are some adjectives I used in just one paragraph of the 1989 Christmas letter to describe Jamison as a toddler. Adorable, friendly, happy, healthy, pleasant, little, delightful, bright, playful, congenial, sensitive, loveable, sweet and irresistible.

I'm sure he was all those things, but... really Stephanie? All in one paragraph?

Oh there's more. This is a small look at what appeared in another letter, "Genevieve completed Suzuki Piano Book One, and is beginning to study Beethoven sonatinas... Jamison played his first Suzuki piano recital... Alexandra graduated to a bigger violin.... Jamison turned three in March... Alexandra lost her first two teeth... Alexandra progressed to Suzuki Violin Book Two... Genevieve had two stitches in her chin... Brooklynne had surgery for a hernia... she walked at 10 months... Jamison went to nursery school... a weekend at Cypress Hills... Ron took Jamison fishing... hot summer days by the pool... vacations in Calgary and Edmonton... Stephanie became involved in the Home and School Association, Suzuki Parents Association, Newcomers Club, ladies Bible study, playgroup moms..." and on and on and on....

Many of our wonderful friends have graciously told me they enjoyed our creative letters, but now as I look back, those letters were out of control! It was all about us and we and our and me and my and I. If a reader looked carefully, they could find Christ tucked in there somewhere between hockey and music lessons, just after summer holidays and before ski trips. I know most Christmas letters are the perfect opportunity to send an update to friends. An update, not a thesaurus/info package/short story contest entry.

These letters went on like this for years. Then I think God had had enough. He tenderly softened our hearts enough that we chose to change. We loved Jesus and had each made a personal commitment to Him. But we were standing on the shoreline with Him. He was ready to take us into deeper waters with Himself and we needed to take some steps of faith. He used our Bible-believing church, some dear followers of Jesus Christ and the ministry of His Hill Bible School in Texas to point us to Himself. We became a family lively and alive in Christ.

In some ways those letters still read a lot like overdone infomercials filled with enough facts to make your eggnog curdle. God still had a lot of work to do in our lives. Here's a look at the letter I wrote soon after I allowed some change to occur in my life. Hmm....

The Gladysz Family Christmas 1993

'Twas the night before Christmas cards, and all through our place,
Not a pencil lay idle, let alone the erase.
Our story of '93 comes with God's blessings,
We know that He's with us, without even guessing.
The children were nestled, out there on the prairie,
Saskoil said, "moving time," then we went hairy.
And Steph with some patience said, "Ok, let's pack"
So bye now to Estevan, then Regina- we're back.
Went back to our neighbourhood, back to our school,
the kids were so happy; they know God's no fool.

Away to the golf course, Ron flew like a pro,
played game after game, swinging clubs to and
fro.
The heat of the summer took us back to the east,
for one fun-filled month, we did family and
feast.
So many great family and friends we did see,
we had to be thankful to Him, you'll agree.
The autumn came quickly, so back to routine,
and little Miss Genevieve's now a pre-teen.
She's skating and swimming and piano still
plays,
praise God that her faith still grows stronger
each day.
Alexandra is eight, full of love and compassion,
violin and synchro-swim are both still in fashion.
And then in a twinkle, there's Brooklynne, our
love,
she's happy and healthy, a gift from above.
Don't call her the baby, or littlest one,
she copies them all and plays violin for fun.
As we drew in our breath, just to slow down
the pace,
down the ice comes our Jamison; "hockey" says
his face.
With dad as a coach and three sisters cheering,
there's not much this kindergartener will ever
be fearing.
But all of these children play on one winning
team,
and the rules are clear, it's a biblical theme.
He spoke in His Word, it went straight to our
hearts,
and filled all our lives and set us apart.
And laying down His life for all who accept Him,

*our Jesus is ready to cleanse and forgive sin.
But we heard that angels proclaimed, as they
sang and did bless...*

*"Glory to God in the highest, and on earth peace
among men with whom He is pleased." Luke
2:14*

Well, that letter had a much better focus than
some of the other letters I just took time to re-read.

Most of my busy and bustling letters must
have caused some people to read for a bit, then
take a break, do some Christmas shopping to
relax, and then maybe go back to finish reading
it- if they dared.

One year I composed "An Incredible Christmas
Feast." I wrote about a six-layer Christmas salad
(representing the six of us), roast turkey with
prairie stuffing (life in a prairie city), and holiday
bars for dessert (a look at our special holiday
times as a family). That weird theme makes me
laugh.

In 2000 I highlighted Luke in our letter. Luke
wasn't a new addition to the family. He was a
doctor and a writer who lived many years ago.
God caused me to make room in my heart and
in my Christmas letter for the profound words
that Luke had penned about 1900 years ago. I
took what he wrote in Luke 2:1-20 and copied it
word for word in my letter. Whether or not it's the
Christmas season, this would be a good time for
you and me to pick up our Bibles and read that
passage aloud.

I was so thankful for those words that God had
written for all of us centuries ago, that became

my Christmas letter of 2000. No detailed summary of the year, no play by play of hockey games, no mention of instruments and medals or what I wore on my birthday. Jesus is the reason for Christmas, pure and simple. As Christ became our focus in life, I prayed this reality would be evident in my Christmas letters. Girlfriends, I'm so thankful God never gives up on me.

A few years ago God stirred in me to write the Top Ten Blessings from 2004. It was almost impossible to choose only ten. Another December He gave me The Gift of the Homecoming to write which was seven short paragraphs about the joy of being together at home for the holidays, and the true meaning of Christmas.

As I prepared to write the letter of 2007, I vividly recall the Lord bringing the word "tradition" to my mind many times. So I wrote The Tradition, a short letter that described our Christmas Day traditions. I'll share the closing paragraph with you. Do you want to get yourself another coffee first? I can wait.

Friends, all other traditions pale in comparison to the true Christmas story. After all, this one has been honoured for over 2,000 years. And without it we'd have nothing to celebrate on December 25th. But God created and gave us the tradition of celebrating Jesus, not only on Christmas day but every day- for all of us, because He loves us. It's His tradition.

I can see that in past letters I spent too much energy on frivolous facts and not enough on Who has given me energy, ideas and new life. Creativity is a great thing, but we need to acknowledge Christ as our blessing rather than the blessings themselves. As He continues to pour out His grace into our family, He also shows me how to turn those blessings back to Him in praise.

And only God could have guided me to and through a letter from a couple of years ago. I was considering writing something with a unique twist on a Christmas carol. Then one morning... *(gasp) I have an idea!*

I began to pour over the famous and favourite old carol, Joy to the World! My finished product was a careful look at some of the lyrics in this sacred song and how they apply to our lives today. I also played a question and answer game with my family. I asked them to answer this question. "What does the phrase... 'And wonders of His love' mean to you?" Each of their responses was so deeply personal- a reflection of six personal relationships with Jesus. Oh girlfriends, God is good.

At the beginning of this chapter I talked about being satisfied with my confession of writing too many obnoxious Christmas letters. But the Lord had a better plan in mind for me. Much to my surprise, as I wrote this chapter, Jesus gave me a good look at the tender journey that He's gently taken me on over the years, as He led me to the cross via the manger.

Finally, I feel the need to personally apologize to anyone who's suffered through years of my letters looking for some real meaning. If you're

reading this book and you were ever a recipient of one of my crazy Christmas letters, please accept my apology for these family infomercials, detailed to death diaries and my prideful long-windedness, all in the name of Christmas letters. I apologize for taking you through the daily minute-by-minute intensity of life with four children less than seven years apart in age. After all, we were the ones who decided to have four children, not you. If you had wanted to know what it was like to raise four children, I suppose you would've had four of your own!

Ten

Bad Coffee, Members and Embers

**Psalm116:13 I shall lift up the cup of salvation
And call upon the name of the LORD.**

Bad Coffee

I've always loved teenagers.

Even as a little girl playing house, I pretended to be the mom of teenagers, as well as the mother of the baby dolls I rocked. Perhaps when we delight ourselves in the Lord as innocent young children, He chooses to give us the desires of our hearts many years later.

Did God look down at me from the balconies of heaven and say, "Hmm... she loves teenagers so much that I'll give her a season in her life when she has four children who will all be teenagers at the same time?" Whatever the case, that's what He did and those teen years were superb!

I'm neither crazy nor a super mom, although I believe the dictionary definition of "mothering" should include the words "extreme sport." Please don't put this book down thinking, "that's not me," because God may want to stir up your creativity through something He's done in our family. Like the morning He gave me a *(gasp) I have an idea!* moment in a Calgary diner.

Ron and I were on our way to a golf tournament. We stopped at a breakfast diner with some friends with whom I felt I could relax and be myself. Upon being seated I noticed the children at the table beside us were colouring, so I asked our server if I could also have some crayons and a colouring sheet. It's at times like that when my husband looks at me and shakes his head. I can't remember the server's reaction, but I did get my crayons. As I began colouring, with my bad cup of coffee at my side, I noticed something remarkable about the picture. Now hold that thought for a few minutes. Maybe you'd like to get yourself a cup of coffee? Good coffee I hope.

Earlier that summer we'd purchased a trampoline for our backyard. The children were older and it was an item we all agreed would provide fun, exercise and entertainment for the many teens that hung out in our backyard. And I do mean many teens. Sometimes 30 or 40 on a nice summer day. Remember, I love teenagers. The trampoline turned out to be a great toy, which filled one corner of our backyard.

Teens bounced on it from morning until midnight. We implemented a 12:00 a.m. no-bounce curfew because the echo of the creaking springs and laughter resounded through our quiet suburban neighbourhood. Trampolines were the hot new item in the summer of 1998 and it seemed like our backyard was the place to be, which thrilled us. I served more ice tea, lemonade, popcorn and chips that summer than Costco could stock. I'd do a dishwasher load of glasses every night and Ron watched the woodpile disappear into ashes each evening. You can read more on that in "Members and Embers" later in this chapter.

Now I suppose you are wondering how this all fits together- colouring in Calgary and rebounding in Regina? Well girlfriends that's the exciting part. All I was expecting that day in Calgary was a round of golf, many lost balls and a breathtaking view of God's handiwork of the Canadian Rockies. But God suddenly turned my attention to what would eventually become a kingdom matter.

You'll recall that I noticed something interesting about my colouring sheet. It was a picture of a trampoline and three little egg shaped people jumping happily. Ideas began to dance in my head. The next time our server came by with coffee I smiled and politely asked her if I could have a few more colouring sheets for my children. Ron stared at me with that "what are you up to now" look, but he also recognized my "I'll tell you later" smile. He knew quite clearly I had an idea.

I can blame the bad golf game that day on the fact that I was preoccupied with a divine idea moment. That, and the bad coffee with which I started my day. I couldn't wait to get back to Regina to make copies of these colouring sheets. We were about to host the first ever Summer Colouring Contest! I knew it from the instant I laid eyes on the picture of those adorable little egg people jumping on their trampoline, just like all those teens in our backyard. I was certain those sheets were made for our summer of 1998! Twelve years later, I still marvel at this fun little idea.

Within days of returning home from Calgary, I'd made a few dozen copies of the sheets, found every coloured marker in the house and set up two tables of colouring stations- one in the family room and one on the picnic table. Then I eagerly waited for the teenagers to arrive. And they did, looking rather inquisitively at this new activity. God bless all those teens that visited our home that summer. They began to colour before I'd finished outlining the instructions.

The Summer Colouring Contest was simple. Participants could enter as many times as they wanted and they also had complete artistic freedom to decorate their sheets in any fashion. Completed entries were to be placed on my desk. The contest closed at the end of the summer and prizes would be awarded on a specified evening. Again, ladies, I get so excited as I replay this in my mind. Remembering those teenagers enthusiastically colouring in our backyard and at the coffee table, still fills my heart with praise to God for His goodness in our lives.

I don't think I need to get into details with you about all the other things they could've been doing on a ho-hum evening. Lazy summer nights have been known to brew less desirable pastimes. You know what I'm talking about. What an honour it was to use the home that God has given us to provide a safe and fun environment in which young people could relax. Their parents, many of whom were our friends, appreciated this option. They'd often send over bags of junk food as thanksgiving offerings. I love my friends. I love Jesus.

Can you picture 20 or 30 young teens sitting around tables in our home talking quietly, or at times not so quietly, colouring, sharing markers (like in kindergarten), complimenting each other and carefully looking over their work? This went on night after night for about a month, until the end of the summer when we planned a special evening of awards and prizes.

Everyone came on results night. I'm not sure what kind of prizes they were expecting, but I know I made a good run to my local dollar store and stocked up on fine treasures of all kinds.

I vividly remember two particular young men who hung around our home regularly. They arrived a few minutes late on judgment night, but in time to hand in a few more masterpieces. It seemed like they weren't satisfied with the numerous others they had already submitted. These creative young minds had not only coloured their sheets, but had also glued fresh grass around the bottom and real twigs on the edges to represent our yard. Whatever these young men did, from wakeboarding to snowboarding to jumping on the trampoline- and now entering a colouring contest- they did it with gusto.

Girls, I have to tell you, we had hundreds of entries in our colouring contest. Ron and I had quite a task ahead of us in judging these little pieces of art. We even recruited help from our younger children, Jamison and Brooklynne. The teens ate and jumped and socialized until late in the evening when we finally emerged with armfuls of colouring sheets and prizes. I think we were able to award everyone a silly prize in all sorts of categories- most elaborate, simple, meticulous, realistic, imaginative, colourful, the first entry, the final entry, the most entries by one person and on and on.

When we were finally done, it didn't seem right to throw away all those pictures and memories. So the next morning, with a good cup of coffee in my hand, I hung each piece of art in the basement family room where all these teenagers would soon hang out once the cool fall weather blew into our backyard.

All this transpired because of a breakfast date, a bad cup of coffee and an idea moment from the Lord. What about you? Would you allow the Lord to show you how He can work in unique ways through you? Even when it seems a bit out of the ordinary? How can He use you to influence young people He brings across your path? How can God use your home to be a great arena for loving children of any age? I suggest you go over that with Him, while I take a short break to make some Italian pizza bread that I call "A Pizza Party in your Mouth," something I made often for our teen visitors. I'll share that recipe with you in a bit.

Members

I guess you could say we had dozens of "members" who hung around our home the summer of the colouring contest. As I'm sure you've come to realize, we enjoyed every minute of opening our home to them, always looking for opportunities to point them to Christ through hospitality.

There was a problem however. I was going through far too many plastic cups and the glass ones were disappearing. I needed an idea to solve this dilemma, but didn't expect to find one in my local department store one sunny afternoon. Mason jar glasses by the case! They were less than a dollar a glass, rugged and the perfect size. I gasped and got an idea. God was with me in the housewares aisle. After all, He was the One bringing all those teenagers to our home. I purchased two cases and proudly brought them home.

That night, when the teens began to arrive, I redirected them away from the kitchen and over to a small table where I'd set up the cups. But after a few nights I could see that I hadn't bought anywhere near enough glasses. First thing in the morning I headed back to the store for a few more boxes of mugs.

But yet another small problem arose. Ahh... such is life. I was still going through far too many cups because our guests kept misplacing their glasses. Hmm... I needed another idea. After a quick gasp I headed to my craft room where I found a box of different colours of fabric paint. After some experimenting in my test kitchen, the problem was solved and I was elated. God makes me smile.

By the time the teenagers arrived for their next gathering, I had a craft table set up for them. Remember, these were the same young people who loved to colour. The instructions were also as simple as the colouring contest. They could each decorate and personalize their own cup using fabric paint, and ta-da, every time they came over their glass was ready for a night of fun.

I was truly in awe of God as I watched these loveable teens spend their summer nights decorating their glasses. It was very interesting to observe them. Each cup was as unique as the person who crafted it and their personality was clearly reflected in their artwork. Many of the girls had carefully planned, neat work and used coordinating colours. Some of the boys had their glasses done in about five minutes and were back on the trampoline.

I've shared all this with you, dear friend, not only as a homey story, but to point you to Christ as you seek His purpose for your home as a venue for ministry. The ideas you get from Him may have more kingdom value than you could ever plan. So I urge you, allow Him to work in your heart and in your home.

Warning: Don't wash painted cups in the dishwasher. The paint will be washed away with last night's dinner. Hand wash in warm, not hot, soapy water. Dishwashers don't easily digest fabric paint. Trust me, I know.

And about those Embers...

My parents had no idea of the significance of what they were doing when they gave us their portable fire pit. They had no idea how God would take that well-used piece of iron and use it for His glory. But come to think of it, 2,000 years ago God showed us He could use iron nails to give us eternal life. We should never underestimate the power of the Almighty.

When my parents renovated their backyard, we inherited their old fire pit. We'd never had one so Ron was careful to place it in a safe location. Far from the trampoline, away from fences and not too close to the trees. That's rather difficult in a suburban yard, but Ron and Jamison took the challenge and won. When their project was completed, the fire pit looked like it had always belonged in the yard, adding a unique and calming atmosphere to the grounds.

At that time, backyard fire pits weren't a common item in our neighbourhood, so little did we know it would become a focal point of the backyard and a highlight of most evenings. After a long day of work, school and activities, we all found there was something soothing about relaxing by the bursting fire. The fire pit became a hit not only with our family, but with our friends as well.

I wish you could've seen what God gave us the privilege of experiencing. Groups of young people colouring, painting cups, chatting on the deck, lounging on the trampoline and gathered by the fire engrossed in conversation. Many of those times around the glowing embers stimulated heartfelt sharing and a stillness before the Lord. Even when Ron and I managed to book adult time around the fire, we found that we had very special times with Jesus and our friends.

I always appreciated the kind-hearted musician who'd saunter in with his guitar ready to lead the group in campfire or worship songs. One summer I looked out the kitchen window and my heart was filled with joy. The young man playing the guitar was our son Jamison. During those times I prayed that the neighbours could sense the sweet aroma of worship to the Almighty God that rose up from those quiet but passionate voices by the fading embers.

There's nothing more I can add, but to say that a fire pit, even the most basic one you can find or build is a wonderful idea. God doesn't need to use elaborate or costly toys in order to work in our lives. I've seen Him use a simple fire pit, iced tea and fabric paint for His glory. Too bad it's the middle of February and -25° C. or we'd be out by the fire tonight with some lemonade.

And now, for your dining pleasure, here's the Italian Pizza Bread recipe I promised.

A Pizza Party in your Mouth

1 cup warm water
2 T. honey
2 T. yeast
3 cups flour (I use some white and some whole wheat)
1 t. salt

Topping it off

1/4 cup or so of Italian dressing
1/4 cup parmesan cheese
1/2 cup grated mozzarella cheese

fresh ground pepper
a hit of dried oregano, basil, thyme

Dissolve honey and yeast in warm water. Let this bubble up until it is foamy. Combine the salt and flour. Add the flour to the liquid a little bit at a time. Knead away. You may need to add a bit more warm water to make a nice smooth dough. Cover it and let it rise for about an hour on a floured surface. Punch down the dough, then roll it into a 10-inch round and place it on a pizza brick or pizza pan sprinkled with cornmeal. (Of course an easier option is to purchase some pre-made pizza shells.) Spread on the Italian dressing, and then top it with spices and cheeses. Bake at 425° F. for about 10 minutes or until it looks done. This pizza serves anywhere from two to six hungry teens, depending on gender and size.

I can't tell you how often this recipe saved me when a bunch of hungry teens showed up in the kitchen. I'd always keep a few pizza dough rounds in my freezer, ready to be topped and baked. A secret: This ready-to-go snack made me look like a culinary genius in a teenager's eyes. That's a good thing.

Eleven

Talking time, Tuck in time

**Deuteronomy 6:5-7 You shall love the LORD
your God with all your heart and with all
your soul and with all your might. These
words, which I am commanding you today,
shall be on your heart. You shall teach them
diligently to your sons and shall talk of them
when you sit in your house and when you
walk by the way and when you lie
down and when you rise up.**

Talking Time

Those tender verses of Scripture, breathed
by the very mouth of God cause me to tear
up whenever I read them. I don't think I've ever
read that passage without experiencing the well-
known lump-in-thy-throat syndrome. You know
the one I mean.

The Lord first used these verses to influence
my life long before our children were even pre-
teens. In May of 1994 I wrote the word "wow" in my

90

Bible beside this passage, one which the Lord has taken me back to on numerous occasions. Each time I read this He shows me the significance of this command and the direction we should take as we parent our little flock. Who says children don't come with a manual?

Genevieve began to speak at a very early age. In full sentences. It really seemed to her dad and me that she bypassed baby talk and unintelligible sounds. She went straight to sentences. Maybe I'm exaggerating a bit, but only a bit. So as a stay-at-home mom I had no choice but to have a lot of talking time with her. But during our talking time, without even realizing, I was following the guidelines assigned to me in Deuteronomy 6.

Talking time was great, but I wished we'd had more tuck-in time. You see, Genevieve never slept. You know that toddler- the catnapper. Five minutes in the car seat, seven minutes in the stroller, two minutes in the high chair. Interestingly though, she was the happiest, most darling little thing ever. Ron and I were thankful for Genevieve's cheerful spirit, because she was only 20 months old when her sister was born.

Girlfriends, God knows what He's doing. He gave us Alexandra who slept 20 hours a day during the first year of her little life! During my pregnancy, I hadn't even prayed for a baby who would sleep. I don't think I even realized that some babies slept. So what do you do with a busy, energetic, inquisitive, chattering, very awake toddler when it's time to nurse your baby?

Once again my Lord showed up and gave me one of His best ideas. We'd have talking time on the "talking stool." My grandfather had built me a small 1970's-orange, upholstered stool, which sat in one corner of the family room. As soon as Genevieve realized it was feeding time she would immediately drag it over to my side. I can still picture tiny Genevieve huffing and puffing as she pushed the stool over to where I was nursing Alexandra, proudly seating herself on it, sitting up very straight and declaring, "Let's have talking time." This happened every single time. She would also haul over a huge basket of books so when talking time was over, we had reading time. What an adorable sight it was to see this ambitious 20-month-old set us up for quality time together.

Twenty-five years later, I see her God given gift of administration so evident in her life and ministry. The Lord was preparing her since babyhood to become the woman she is today, for His good pleasure. When Genevieve innocently initiated our talking times in the toddler days, that was actually the Lord working in my life gently saying, "Stephanie, you shall talk when you sit in your house..."

One of her favourite topics during talking time was "good girls and boys." Genevieve and I would take turns making statements like, "good girls and boys take a bath." Then Genevieve would say something like, "good girls and boys help mommy." I might have added, "good girls and boys go to the library." And Genevieve may have said, "good girls and boys eat all their vegetables," or "good girls and boys read Bible stories." She could go on for a very long time.

It was a wonderful pastime and I had absolutely no inkling how God would use those times to shape our relationship with each of the children. Ladies, all I can say is, if the Lord your God has put little ones in your life, find yourselves a grandpa to build you a talking stool. Wait and see what He does with some wood. After all, He once constructed a glorious manger and a redeeming cross.

When we grew out of the talking stool days, God transitioned us to talking time as we walked to nursery school, drove to a friend's for play day, baked cookies together or during bath time. Whenever I had the opportunity to chat with the children I did just that. And yes, it was exhausting. But often our conversations would end with a spontaneous little prayer, reminding me from Whom my energy comes.

Tuck-in Time

Talking time and tuck-in time have been a package deal in our home and in my heart since our babies were born.

There's always been a need in *me* to tuck each of our children into bed every single night. In my opinion it was wrong for any of them to go to sleep without being tucked in. Notice *I* was the one with this huge need. It was part of the routine- bath time, story time, prayer time and tuck-in time. Even as they grew older and could handle the bedtime regime themselves, I had the unstoppable motherly urge to always be there to hug and tuck. Bless their little hearts. I can still hear them announce from their rooms, "Mom, I'm ready to be tucked in." Ahh... those beautiful words.

In contrast, the most dreaded words I could've ever heard come from a bedroom were, "Good night, I'm going to bed and I don't need you to tuck me in, it's ok." Are you kidding me? I *needed* to tuck them in. It was the mother gene in me that caused me to dash up the stairs to prevent that poor child from going to bed untucked.

In the teen years, there were many times I'd head up to bed while they were still doing homework, so I'd ask one of them to tuck me in. (Our poor children.) Someone would always show up by my bedside. But after I'd been tucked in and we'd gotten a laugh over that, I was never surprised when that teen would flop down on the bed and open up his or her heart and thoughts to me. Now as young adults, when they come home for a visit... you guessed it, I still want to tuck them in.

I don't want you to think that Ron's missing the tuck-in gene. Often when I'm done my tuck-in ritual, he'll slip in for a dad moment. His fatherly tenderness radiates as he tucks in our children, and when he prays for them I hear Deuteronomy 6:5-7 come alive in his life and in our home.

You're a wise woman. You know that so much more comes from those times than just a hug and a tuck. As I sit on the edge of the bed, the busyness of the day dims like the light in the bedroom and our best conversations softly transpire. They know they have my undivided attention. They know I care and this sacred time belongs to them.

My heart is full as I read those verses from Deuteronomy 6 again. "... talk of them when you sit in your house and when you walk by the way and when you lie down..." School issues, girl situations, growing up questions, spiritual matters. There were no limits on topic or time. The questions of life were piling up for them and those took priority over my laundry pile that could wait until morning. Growing children can't wait for us to work them into our agendas. They keep growing.

During our talking times and tuck-in times Brooklynne and I earnestly prayed together as we considered a new school for junior high. Genevieve and I saw the hand of God lead her to Bible school after many nights of talking and tucking. Alexandra and I had countless heart to heart discussions about the choices facing teenagers who were in the world, but not of the world. But the most unforgettable tuck-in time occurred one night with Jamison.

Our healthy nine-year-old little hockey player had suddenly been diagnosed with a mass in his abdomen. And by suddenly, I mean he was at hockey practice in the afternoon and 24 hours later doctors were preparing him for surgery to remove the mysterious mass that was sitting between his kidney and aorta.

He was able to spend the night before his surgery at home. That evening the Lord used Jamison to point me to Christ in an incredible and powerful way. It was one of the most profound God-moments of my life.

We'd finished praying and as I was about to tuck him in, Jamison sat up on the top bunk of his bed and calmly announced to me, "Mommy, I know Jesus can heal me." I looked up at my little boy and felt God pierce my heart with those simple, but truthful words uttered in child-like faith. Through my tears, and in awe of God I said, "Yes Jamison, you're right, I know He can." God did heal Jamison and with all my heart and soul and mind and strength, I sing praises to Him for that. Throughout the weeks that followed Jamison's surgery, I clung to the Lord and to the truth that was spoken that night. We had so much to thank God for, including the gift of His mighty presence at tuck-in time.

One night during our usual tuck-in time, four-year-old Brooklynne asked me to sit on the floor by her bedside until she fell asleep. I was about to list off a great number of reasons why I couldn't do that, when she interrupted me suggesting that I read my Bible while I sat there. Now that was a great idea moment! How could I decline that precious offer? I grabbed my Bible and settled onto the floor by her bed. This ritual went on for a few months, but friends, what could be better for a little child than to watch her dad or mom reading God's Word by her side as she falls asleep?

I relished this quiet time before the Lord, and often I'd continue reading for quite a while after she'd fallen asleep. It was during one of those times that the Lord guided me back to this passage in Deuteronomy, meeting us in our need to make so many parenting decisions.

More recently Brooklynne's favourite part of tuck-in time was a back rub as she drifted off to sleep. I knew she'd soon be leaving home to go to college, so I took advantage of those times to give her a bit of a massage. Undoubtedly, the Lord led us into good conversations as she faded off to sleep. I miss those cherished times. Girlfriends, as I walk by her empty room now, I long for the chance to give her a little back rub. I urge you with all my heart to enjoy your children while you have them in the nest, because from the moment they're born they start flapping those little wings in preparation for the big flight.

Are you diligently teaching God's commands to your children when you sit at home or during your leisure time with them? That's the command for parents in Deuteronomy. How does that play out in your family life? Would you inquire of the Lord and look to Him to inspire you with His ideas? As I look back over the years, I see God in our talking times- driving to hockey tournaments, walking by the lake, sitting on the beach, relaxing on the backyard swing, making dinner, picking weeds, coffee dates (that's prime talking time), baking and even at the grocery store.

Last week, Alexandra text messaged me from Calgary saying she missed me and *needed* to grocery shop with me. She didn't really require my help in the supermarket. I knew that meant she wanted us to connect as mother and daughter for some talking time while leisurely strolling through the market. And so Deuteronomy 6 comes alive in the grocery store... when you walk by the way.

A few more things from the manual

I have many sisters in Christ whose lives glorify the Lord. By God's grace they've raised children who love the Lord, fear the Lord and walk closely with the Lord. I asked our children to give me the names of women in their lives who've raised what I call Mark 12:30 children. I wasn't in the least bit surprised with the names that showed up in my inbox one day. So I asked these women, who I also love and admire, the following questions.

What are some verses that the Lord used to guide, direct and encourage you as you raised your children? What more can you share about how God used these verses?

My long time friend Sharon in Regina answered... I instantly thought of what may seem at first a strange verse to pick, but it has been my prayer and focus for many years. Of course there are many verses, but this one stands out to me.

"For David, after he had served the purpose of God in his own generation, fell asleep, and was laid among his fathers and underwent decay." Acts 13:36

The phrase that has been my prayer for our children, emphasizes that they would "serve the purpose of God in their generation"- not my purpose, not their own purpose, not the world's purpose, but God's purpose. They are not their own for they have been bought with a price; they are not ours, they have been loaned to us; they are His, put here at this time and in this place, to fulfill God's purpose for them.

Another verse that has been equally important to my husband and me is Acts 4:13 (NIV). "When they saw the courage of Peter and John and realized that they were unschooled, ordinary men, they were astonished and they took note that these men had been with Jesus."

This verse has really directed the focus of our home schooling and parenting. Worldly activities do not count; what counts is that my children (and we) have been with Jesus. For "without Him I can do nothing;" yet with Him, "I can do all things through Him who strengthens me."

My sweet southern friend Patsy shared... The verse that I prayed for our kids nightly is the one you mentioned, to love the Lord with all your heart, soul, mind and strength. Another passage that the kids and I memorized is Psalm1. It is a wonderful chapter. My prayer for the kids was for them to be solidly founded on the Word of God. I wanted to be faithful to lead them to the Lord and now it seems that they are going to the Lord on their own, for which we are so thankful. There is NO other foundation to build upon.

My special friend Doris in Meadow Lake told me... I was so blessed to be able to stay at home and enjoy the many years my children were young, preschoolers, as well as in their formative years of school. A Scripture that I continually kept before me was Deuteronomy 6:5-9. (NIV): "Love the LORD your God with all your heart and with all your soul and with all your strength. These commandments that I give you today are to be upon your hearts. Impress them on your children. Talk about them when you sit at home and when you walk along the road, when you lie down and when you get up. Tie them as symbols on your hands and bind them on your foreheads. Write them on the doorframes of your houses and on your gates."

Oh, how we longed for our children to know God's presence in ALL aspects of their lives. He wants to be an integral part of everything we are, everywhere we go, everything we do and say- He is ready to bless us in every intricate part of our lives.

Another Scripture that we often kept at the forefront as our children got older, was 1 Corinthians 10:23. NIV. "Everything is permissible"- but not everything is beneficial. "Everything is permissible"- but not everything is constructive. "Nobody should seek his own good, but the good of others." We often gave that Scripture to our children as they faced decisions regarding "choices" of activities, movies, music etc.

There were many other Scriptures that encouraged me as a mom- to pray, asking for protection for my children from my own sins, to "let go and let God" … aren't we blessed to be women of faith in a God who is aware, is faithful and full of grace and mercy! I often look at my children and am in awe of what God has done in their lives.

Where is your Deuteronomy 6:7 happening? I would like to suggest you turn off the television, shut down your computer, step away from your briefcase, leave the dishes, put away the remote, and communicate with your children... because they could be in their rooms researching colleges, planning trips to far off lands and making a packing list. And soon those bedrooms could be empty. Remember Chapter 2?

Twelve

Baubles and Books

**Hebrews 10:24 ... and let us consider how to
stimulate one another to love
and good deeds...**

I'm excited. I'm smiling.

Today's a holly jolly day because I'm writing about several ideas the Lord gave me that are each wrapped around my favourite time of the year. The Christmas season. Sometimes I get so thrilled over new ideas that I find myself wishing they'd occurred sooner, but since the Lord's in charge, I need to trust Him for His agenda. They have a popular saying in Texas. "Don't Mess With Texas." Girls, let's not mess with God.

Baubles

Christmas is the perfect time for cultivating new ideas that help to make this season of rich traditions even more grand. The circumstances surrounding the birth of this idea are unclear, but

I do recall it happened, with gusto, a few weeks before Christmas about five years ago. And like I've said, I'm always open to a new playful idea.

One frosty morning I got it into my head that the children needed a sibling ornament exchange.

What fun! The older girls were both living in Texas, and the younger two were still at home. I decided the Texans would exchange ornaments and the Canadians would be the other pair. The guidelines were straightforward- purchase or hand-make an ornament for your partner. Creativity was strongly encouraged. The exchange would be done when we were all together at home a few days before Christmas. Much to my merry holiday joy, the children were enthusiastic about the newly proposed venture. Bless them.

And what better way to have celebrated this idea than to have a commemorative "First Annual Gladysz Sibling Christmas Ornament Exchange Party" featuring a little shortbread and eggnog when everyone finally arrived home. As we all gathered in the family room, I could see that the children were anxious to give out their carefully planned, personal baubles.

Within a few short minutes a magenta feathered bird, a delicate red and gold mesh ball, a vibrant pink velvety treasure, and a funky looking black and white ornament were all unveiled. You can guess which one was Jamison's. That black and white ornament began a tradition for him. Many of the ones he's received since then are in that colour scheme.

Each year I change the bauble-giving pairs and watch as the ornaments become more personalized. A few years ago Brooklynne had spent some extended time in Texas. So when Genevieve had her as a partner, she gave her an armadillo ornament. Yes ma'am, you can most definitely find armadillo Christmas ornaments in the Lone Star State. And then when Jamison attended Bible school he and Genevieve were paired up. He does things in the most creative ways- her Christmas ball was about 18 inches in diameter. Big, like Texas.

A few years ago Alexandra and Jamison were paired up as the Calgarians. She must've recalled the gigantic ball he'd given to Genevieve and she gave him a 12 inch ball, following the black and white theme. Jamison was working at the well known coffee shop that many of us love to frequent far too often (the one whose name boldly advertises the biblical sign in Matthew 2 that the magi saw in the east...) so appropriately he gave her an ornament from there and saved himself a few... (ahem)... bucks! Get it?

Genevieve and Brooklynne were paired off as our Texans. Brooklynne, a creative little photographer, took a picture of the chapel at their Bible school and made it into an ornament for Genevieve. Genevieve found her sister a handcrafted wooden Lone Star decoration at a Christmas craft fair in her town. Now can you see why I get so excited? We have so much fun with this idea that's sweeter than a mug of hot chocolate and a coloured marshmallow.

These ornaments annually hang on our family tree, (except for the monstrous ones) but the day will come when I'll package them up and they'll hang on another tree in another home. Until then, we delight in seeing some sibling lovin' on our family tree. This idea has become a much-anticipated touch to our special family times over the holidays. I pray the annual ornament exchange is a sign to our children that God has blessed them with the gift of family, and that it also reminds them to love one another.

Scratch and Sniff

Almost from the moment we brought our children home from the hospital, reading to them became a priority. We had all types of books in every corner of our home, but some of our favourite ones were those that proclaimed the truth about Christmas. We also had some that represented good old-fashioned wintertime fun. Even now with a house full of young adults, over the holidays you'll find a stack of children's Christmas books in a corner of our family room.

One Christmas Brooklynne lamented over the lack of scent left in a childhood scratch and sniff book. (I'm not sure if you're with me on this one, but it's a book with scented stickers on each page that give off a particular fragrance when scratched. For instance, a pine cone sticker smells like a piney forest, and a candy cane sticker smells minty.) We have an adorable book called The Sweet Smell of Christmas that little fingers have scratched for 26 years. Brooklynne expressed her sadness that the stickers no longer smelled no matter how hard she scratched.

I don't think there's ever been a Christmas that at some point I haven't gasped and exclaimed, "I have an idea!" It's the time of year for sparkling ideas to twinkle and shine. I know God used Brooklynne's innocent observation that December day to give me an idea that would leave the children all speechless and teary-eyed on Christmas Eve. (I'm not exaggerating.) Once again, I have to declare that every good and perfect gift is from above. Amen?

My mission was to hunt down four new copies of The Sweet Smell of Christmas and present one to each child for Christmas. Why I begin such tasks in mid December, I don't know. Can you relate? To my amazement, it wasn't long before I had four copies of The Sweet Smell of Christmas, with fresh new stickers just waiting to be scratched and sniffed.

I was beside myself with excitement when the time came to give the books to the children. We usually exchange one little gift on Christmas Eve and I knew which gifts I'd be giving.

Our unsuspecting young adult children looked a bit puzzled at my enthusiasm as I waited for them to open their gifts. All six of us had tears in our eyes that Christmas Eve around the fire. I vividly recall the intimate silence in the family room as the children realized they held a piece of their childhood in their hands. They were surprised and delighted to receive their own new copy of this favourite childhood book. I could see memories flooding their minds. (I'm really not exaggerating this time.) The brief silence was suddenly interrupted with jubilant comments such as, "these are brand new and we each get one!" and

"I'm not going to scratch the stickers so the smell doesn't go away!" and "I can't believe you could find this book after all these years!" It was a perfect moment in my life.

Those were the most significant gifts I gave that year. Each year as winter approaches, I seek out four new copies of another book from our Christmas library to give out on December 24th at around 8:30 p.m. while nibbling on nuts and bolts.

Yes indeed, the Lord has the best ideas and I thank Him for imparting them to me and for His Word that says to stimulate one another to love and good deeds. As I consider this verse, (which I should do more often) my mind wonders and wanders a bit.

Because of God's glorious grace in my life, I love to show love to the *one anothers* in my life. I delight in the manifold ways to share Christ with the world outside our home. You know what I mean. Muffins for a new neighbour. Dinner for a family in crisis. These are all good things that God has created, but I find myself asking Him to take me deeper with Him in this area. What I'm trying to say is that I want to hear and obey Jesus as He shows me how to abundantly love the *one anothers* in my life. Whether it's meals on heels or a tasty little bake 'n take, I want Jesus to be my all in all.

Four young authors and a book

An unassuming plain, black, hardcover book sits beside me on my desk. Inside it you'll find photographs, journaling and artwork. It features a few stories, an interview, some poetry and a series of haikus. Each page looks different and there seems to be no apparent theme. Some portions are hand written and others are printed on fine gold paper. One page looks whimsical and another looks reverent. It's Mom's Christmas Book.

When I read it a variety of emotions percolate in me- I laugh hysterically at one page, another causes my heart to melt as I read about the joy of romance. And yet another page leads me to reflect on the unrivaled love of Christ. At first glance this book looks and sounds rather random, but that's far from true.

By now, you know exactly what I'm about to say. In December 2006 I had a *(gasp) I have an idea!* moment from the Lord. It may have happened as I blew the dust off the Christmas books I read to the children when they were little or perhaps the idea struck me as I counted down the days until they returned home for the holidays. I really don't remember because, like you, I have a lot going on in my head and life in December. But as I've said, God knows exactly what He is up to.

Although I was bursting with enthusiasm over what I spontaneously named Mom's Christmas Book, I caught my breath long enough to let God show me His desires and plans for this treasure. I knew the best way to share this sparkling Christmas idea with the children was through MMMM. (See Chapter 2. The memo has become a great tool of communication.) I couldn't type fast enough when I finally I announced "Mom's Christmas Book."

I presented them with the idea of a book of stories, poetry or photographs related to Christmas or a significant event from the past year. The children were invited to submit one piece to the book and to exercise complete artistic freedom to communicate their story. Some pages looked quite basic and others were very elaborate.

There were three things I asked the Lord for regarding Mom's Christmas Book. Number one: I wanted God to give me a peek into the hearts of my children. Number two: I really wanted to see how Christ had been shaping their lives. Number three: I wanted to know how Christ was working His will in them. The plan was to circulate the book among the children each December so they could enter their offering for the year, thus creating a perpetual treasure.

Oh girlfriend, I wish you could see my book. It has Jesus all over it, which captivated me right from the start.

The first entry was from Genevieve who chose the powerful words from Isaiah 9:6. Words that were printed on glimmering paper, but the message was more precious than gold. "For a child will be born to us, a son will be given to us; and the government will rest on His shoulders; and His name will be called Wonderful Counselor, Mighty God, Eternal Father, Prince of Peace." Then Genevieve wrote some of her own thoughts regarding the passage and how it related to her life in 2006. I praise God for the life He gives to our children.

Alexandra wrote a piece called Christmas in May, the true love story of boy meets girl, which God had written that year for her and her boyfriend, Chris. It was a reminder that God's blessings and precious gifts come in any season. I praise God for the love stories He's writing for all our children. Who needs to hire a wedding planner when we already have the presence of The Almighty Wedding Planner in our lives?

Brooklynne opted for a blend of poetry and photography. That year she had developed a keen interest in photography. Her offering was a nine stanza takeoff on 'Twas the Night Before Christmas, making it her own as she turned the focus away from the reindeer and onto the One who reigns. Her photos were dynamic black and white winter pictures of downtown Regina. I praise God for the gifts and abilities He bestows on our children.

Jamison wrote me three haikus that highlighted summertime, family traditions and the joy of living a life in Christ. It's simple, but yet profound. Each year he shares a bit more of his heart through his poetry and sensitive song lyrics. I praise God that he gave us a son to raise amongst all these girls!

There are pages that include an interview, a look back at family highlights and hilarious quotes from our summer holiday in Denver, a creative version of The 12 Days of Christmas, and lyrics of a song I know I'll hear on an album someday.

I'm picturing this book in about 20 years. Page upon page recording God's fingerprints in the lives of our children and their own families. With a thankful heart I praise God as I read and reread

Mom's Christmas Book, acknowledging that He is the One who makes all things possible.

Don't Mess With Texas Creamed Corn

I know what you're thinking... creamed corn? This is nothing like canned creamed corn. Trust me. Texans serve it as a side dish with barbequed anything, baked beans and peach cobbler. Mmm... I've found this to be the perfect dish to take to a potluck. I can just about guarantee you no one else will show up with creamed corn!

2 lbs. good quality frozen corn
8 oz. cream cheese
1/2 cup butter
1 T. sugar
1/4 cup whipping cream
salt and pepper
1 crock-pot

This is so easy y'all. Place the ingredients into a crock-pot and cook on low for 8 hours, or on high for about 4 hours. Stir and sample often. Serve with lots of pepper. This recipe is easily increased or decreased depending on the crowd you're feeding.

Here's a recipe for a Christmas party in a bowl. From my Mother's tattered, old, brown leather recipe book, established in 1956, I give you the pillar of Christmas comfort food, warm and fuzzy...

Nuts and Bolts 1956

2 cups or so of each of the following... Cheerios, Shreddies, pretzels, Crispex,
2 cups of peanuts, mixed nuts and cashews
Combine all these goodies in a large roaster.

Melt 1 cup of BUTTER! and add 2 T. worcester-shire sauce, a big dash of garlic powder, a very key ingredient... a smaller dash of paprika, chili powder and Cajun spice. Pour this deadly mixture over the cereal and give it all a good toss to bathe the nuts and bolts in luxury. Bake it at 350° F. for about 15 minutes. Stir and bake it again for about 10 minutes. Watch it carefully so it doesn't brown too much. Go ahead and sample it while it cools. Store your nuts and bolts in an airtight container. And I suggest that you hide them from your family... speaking from experience. If no one finds them, they'll last for about a month.

Nuts and bolts are a staple in our home over Christmas. No night by the fire is complete without a tin of them on the coffee table. I love to serve them in festive bowls. I'm smiling right now. Are you?

Thirteen

What do you say...?

**1 Thessalonians 5:18 ... in everything give
thanks; for this is God's will for you
in Christ Jesus.**

I love the darling little sounds babies make.
When our children were tiny babes, we were
captivated by their bubbly sounds that magically
evolved into much anticipated words. The question that was forefront in our minds was, "What
would be the baby's first word?" There was only
one possibility in my mind. Ma-ma. Funny, Ron
didn't look at it that way. He naturally assumed
the baby's first word would be da-da. Hmm....

I had the advantage.

Ron was at work. I was at home with our baby,
so all day long we diligently practiced ma-ma-
ma. He'd come home, graciously offer to bath the
baby and from upstairs I could hear him working
on da-da-da. I think we were just normal parents
with a precious baby who reduced us to a mono-
syllabic vocabulary for a brief period of time. It

didn't really matter how hard each of us played the ma-ma-ma da-da-da game, each baby proved that children have a mind of their own from a very young age. Not one of our four little gifts from heaven spoke ma-ma or da-da as their first word- but all that practicing served as good quality time with our babies.

When Genevieve was a baby my parents had a dog named Goldie. For her first word she translated that name into "aaddee." Alexandra uttered the word "uumm." That meant she wanted something to eat. Sorry Alexandra! Jamison totally overlooked animals and food, and went straight to sports- "aakkee" meant hockey in baby lingo. And Brooklynne, our youngest, didn't surprise us at all when her first word was "uh-oh." After all, her siblings were two, five and six years old when she was born- there were lots of uh-ohs daily. Each of these babies repeated their favourite words, over and over and over each day.

Ladies, we know that these adorable little words eventually come together to make phrases, which merge into full-length sentences and questions. We are all so proud of our children as they achieve these milestones. You know that feeling. However, through these vocal achievements, parents often find themselves battered from morning until night by repetitious questions courtesy of small children. At times we feel like we can't handle one more "mommy why do I have to, mommy how come I can't, mommy can I, mommy when can I, mommy what can I, mommy how can I..."

But have you ever noticed something that we parents do? We turn around and do the same thing to our children. We hound them over and over with one particular question. As I closely examine these phenomena, I'm struck with one particular question with which we bombard our children. You've heard it and I know you've said it to your beloved little ones many times my friend. I'm guilty too. It's the question we just can't resist... "what do you say...?"

Here's the scenario. The setting and conversation requires our child to say thank you to a person, and suddenly we don't trust our child to remember those two simple words. We blurt out the customary question parents feel obligated to extend. We can't help ourselves- it's as universal as baby powder and sleepless nights. We bend down slightly, in a semi-whisper and a pasted smile, with one eye on our child and the other in the direction of the one to be thanked, we question our child, "What do you say...?"

Obviously we are looking for a thank you! We feel we have to prompt the child with that age-old question. How many times have you done exactly what I've described? As for me, I'll be honest... hmm... let's see, four children.... at least 4,000 times. Okay, this time I'm exaggerating, but I think you get my point. We want our children to be gracious, polite, and to express their thanks in an appropriate way at the proper time. Fair enough, that's good parenting and it's our responsibility to raise mannerly children.

But what about us? Should we not practice what we teach? This idea came to me many years ago when we were finally through the "what do you say...?" phase of life. The Lord showed me through His Word that, I too, needed to give thanks in all things, for this was His will for me in Christ. Girlfriend, I have my issues, but saying thank you has always been easy for me. Thank you Jesus, for that.

So I thought I had the basics covered. I was supposed to thank God and thank others. But God began to point out to me that some of the most important "others" in my life were the four precious ones in our flock.

He showed me that I needed to thank them daily, regularly, sincerely, wholeheartedly, unreservedly, cheerfully, passionately, warmly and lovingly. The idea of thanking the children, with those adjectives in the forefront of my mind, took flight in my head and it grew into an active desire. If I was expecting our children to be thankful people, I needed to be much more diligent in showing them my thanks.

That idea sounded more like fun than a chore to me as the Lord showed me unique ways to express my thanks to our children. The most obvious way was to simply say thank you at the right time, complete with eye contact, a smile and using their name. (I read somewhere that the most pleasant sound to a person is his or her name.) I also tried to make it clear why I was thankful. "Jamison, hey buddy, thanks for bringing in all the groceries. You saved me 17 trips from the garage."

Thank you opportunities are all around us girls, and if we choose to live with an attitude of thanksgiving, God will open our eyes to those occasions. This morning, even before I got out of bed I was mulling this chapter over with the Lord, and in His greatness, He took me to three particular instances of thanks. How thankful I am for His leading in my life. All three stories involve recent wedding showers. God's timing is so perfect, girlfriend. He knew I'd be writing this chapter on thanks within days and He set things up for me as only He could do.

This past weekend, a few of us "older women" were having coffee and a chat during a wedding shower at our church for a darling bride named Maria. One dear friend of mine shared with us that she has a loved one in her life who has a very hard time saying thank you. My tender-hearted friend told us how she completely trusts the Lord to lovingly show this young woman how to say thank you. My friend is standing behind the cross of Christ, poised to act in accordance to His will.

We were in church the morning after Maria's shower and when the service ended we found ourselves walking out together. She smiled at me and graciously thanked me for the pasta cookbook and kitchen accessories I'd given her as a shower gift. My mouth dropped and instead of saying "You're welcome," all I could say was, "You remembered exactly what I gave you? Wow, that's amazing." This sweet bride had opened over 60 gifts the day before! I believe this young woman must have grown up with the words thank you.

The Lord reminded me of another shower that I emceed a few years ago. It was for our daughter Genevieve's best friend, Sheena. After opening in prayer I welcomed the large group of women to this special evening. The bride's grandmother shared a beautiful devotion from her heart and we conducted an entertaining mini-interview with the beaming bride. I announced that refreshment time would follow the gift opening.

Before anyone could reach for another glass of pink punch, Sheena stood up and with tears in her gigantic brown eyes, she thanked everyone for attending the shower and planning the night. Then she turned the focus of her thanks to the Lord and the unique role He had assigned to each of these women. She shared how God had used them to mature her over the past 25 years. Girlfriends, Sheena hadn't opened one single gift and yet she was bursting with thanks. As God used this admirable, young woman to teach us all something about thanksgiving, there wasn't a dry eye in the room that night. (Take a minute and visit Sheena's website, *www.sugarweddingcakes.com*. Mmm...)

As I've sought the Lord to give me a thankful heart, He's shown me how to look at life through His eyes and with an attitude of thanksgiving. Throughout the years I've found myself thanking our children for...

- pointing me to Christ.
- having friends who point them to Christ.
- having friends who they can point to Christ.
- attending Bible school, which God has used to open the door for many great conversations with people in our web of influence.
- finally sleeping through the night.
- praying for one another.
- eagerly participating in my wild ideas.
- honouring us as parents.
- being followers of Jesus Christ.
- snuggling with me.
- still wanting to come on family vacations.
- dating men and women who love Jesus.
- allowing me to cry when I needed to.

- sending us love notes.
- surprising Ron and me with homemade dinners.
- telling me (nicely) when to back off.
- consulting us and valuing our opinion, even in their young adult years.
- not staying out all night.
- wanting us to visit them in their homes.
- laughing at the silly e-cards I send.
- allowing me to write about them in this book.
- our unique friendship.
- accepting our discipline, as we disciple them.
- telling me when I have lipstick on my teeth.
- texting, e-mailing, phoning and e-carding me.
- loving us.
- teaching us to take herbs and vitamins.
- suggesting it was time to toss the tacky Christmas/Easter/autumn cardigans (yes, I have sported all of the above).
- golfing with us.
- grocery shopping with me.
- making music in our home.
- helping me (regularly) with my technology issues.
- using their gift of hospitality to honour the Lord.
- exercising their gifts for His kingdom.
- challenging me to know Christ more deeply.
- plucking my eyebrows.
- going to the spa with me.
- being our children.

When I was still in bed this morning thinking about the key points of this chapter, the Lord took me straight to the ending and gave me the idea of how to wrap it all up; with thanks to you for spending your treasured time reading the words I've written. Please accept this personal little thank you note from my desk to your favourite reading chair.

Dearest Friend,

It's been a delight to spend time penning some thoughts from my life and outrageous ideas. I describe it as 100% thrill and 100% fear at the same time, but I believe the Lord has ordained what you've been reading. Knowing your time is valuable, I want to thank you for choosing to spend some of it with me. I pray you'll be inspired to seek the Lord to show you His will and His perfect ideas for your life, and not to be impressed at all with my story, but to be captivated by Christ alone.

You are so special to me, and I'm thankful that He's put us together in this unique way. Thanks again for reading about the Lord in our lives...

With a heart overflowing with gratitude,

Love, Stephanie

Fourteen

On a Mission in the Kitchen

Acts 13:2 While they were ministering to the Lord and fasting, the Holy Spirit said, "Set apart for Me Barnabas and Saul for the work to which I have called them."

When I was a little girl the family kitchen was off limits to me.

From my perch on a kitchen chair, I'd watch quietly, smelling exotic Mediterranean spices, observing delicate culinary procedures and waiting patiently for a small sample of the final product as a reward for my obedience. Cooking was left to the adult women. It was clear to me the best way I could help was to stay out of the way. And so I did.

The result was that when Ron and I were married I couldn't cook a single thing. Nothing. As a young bride-to-be, I vividly recall being captivated by all the intriguing cookbooks I'd received as shower gifts. I kept them in a pile beside my bed and I'd spend hours lingering over each recipe and photograph. I carefully read them in eager anticipation of having my own kitchen that I knew I'd never label as "Kitchen Confidential," like the one in which I'd grown up.

As a brand new bride, I was completely helpless and hopeless in the kitchen. I'll forever be scarred by a picture in my mind of me trying to chop a garlic clove with the skin still on it. I still remember Ron watching me in bewilderment, not saying much. I'm positive he was born with a wooden spoon in his chubby little Polish hand. And I know he held an all-access pass into his family's kitchen.

Bewilderment, I decided, was not what I wanted our children to experience when they walked into their own kitchens as young adults. So, as soon as our children were old enough, I had them by my side in our kitchen, standing safely on a stool, playing with bubbles in the sink or placing cucumbers into the salad bowl. As they got a little older, it was easy to transition into letting them make a salad entirely on their own. It was a big deal for them as they proudly marched their tossed salad over to the table.

During those times by my side on the kitchen stool, my tiny helper learned colours (what colour is the broccoli?), counting (how many pieces of tomatoes are in the salad?), good nutrition (mmm...don't these carrots look yummy?), and as a bonus, we had talking time. You remember Chapter 11.

Speaking of the kitchen stool, I love to set the children up beside me at a sink full of massive bubbles. Dish soap and some water. It's that easy. Bubbles. Truly one the simplest attractions for a toddler. Our children spent hours with me at the kitchen sink splashing around while I got a ton of things done. This idea never let me down.

By the time the children were teens they were quite skilled in the kitchen and I don't mean just the skill of grazing in the refrigerator. They were capable of preparing a basic meal for themselves and a few friends. In our home, the kitchen has always been command central, the hub of activity and a place to gather. Connecting. That was the key ingredient God used that gave me a great idea in the mid 90's as we were planning a week-long family ski trip to British Columbia.

The Lord provided us with a fabulous condominium in Big White, British Columbia on the ski hill, with a view of the mountains and the ski lifts. It was luxurious in all ways, including the price. But God graciously intervened and caused the owners of the condo to rent it to us for a ridiculously low price.

I thanked God for His mercy towards us, but I began to realize I was going to need my family to extend a little grace and mercy to me too, in the culinary zone of this getaway.

As I looked ahead a few weeks to our ski trip, I could imagine our family floating through mounds of fresh powder snow, exhilarated by the sparkling surroundings and laughing merrily as they descended mountains carved by the very hand of God. I could picture this happening without me. Woe is me. I'd be locked up in the condominium kitchen making breakfast, cleaning it up, making lunch, cleaning it up, making hot chocolate, cleaning it up, making dinner, cleaning it up, making bedtime snacks, and cleaning it up.

Then I remembered how I'd always shown our children that time in the kitchen was an opportunity to connect with family and friends. Then I stopped and... *(gasp) I have an idea!*

Teamwork. That was the solution. I convinced our family teamwork is biblical... Barnabas and Saul, Aquila and Priscilla, David and Jonathan, Mary and Joseph. Ron and Jamison, Genevieve and Alexandra, Stephanie and Brooklynne. Cooking teams, what an idea!

I asked every team to provide me with a menu plan and grocery list about a week before our departure date. Each team was responsible for preparing, cooking, serving and cleaning up a couple of breakfasts, lunches, snacks and dinners. Team meetings happened in quiet corners of the house. Menus evolved, siblings eagerly and enthusiastically agreed with one another. Was this really my family? All was well in the world. The concept looked good on paper, but would the whole plan go downhill once we were on the slopes?

Day One: Team Ron and Jamison. Breakfast. They got up and did exactly what they were supposed to do. Lunch. They came off the slopes a half hour before lunch and did their thing again, and when the rest of us were to come in to enjoy the feast, they gave us the signal. You see, one of the chair lifts soared right by the kitchen window of our condominium, so when it was mealtime, one of the chefs gave the wave to the rest of the family, indicating a feast was about to be served.

Cold and hungry we came in to find a hot meal waiting on the table. Dinnertime, same thing. It worked.

Day Two: Team Genevieve and Alexandra. Guess what? It worked again.

Day Three: Ladies, hear what I'm about to tell you. This was the first time on the trip that I set foot in the kitchen. By this point Brooklynne and I were more than ready to pamper our family. Believe me, cooking teams are a grand idea. We all agreed this idea was a keeper and one that we'd implement again on future family vacations.

At the lake, for instance. For many years we've taken a relaxing summer holiday at a cottage by a piney forest in Clear Lake, Manitoba. What a gift those times have been. Even as we planned our treasured summer vacation I could imagine the smell of coffee brewing, crackling bacon and hark... was that Ron's voice calling us for breakfast on the deck? Once again, with cooking teams in place, we enjoyed our times together as a family- sizzling at the beach and by the barbeque. By night we roasted hotdogs over an open fire and by day we looked like hotdogs as we opened fire on the golf course. We played bocce ball by the beach. Since some historians believe bocce ball has Roman roots, I insisted we all speak with thick Italian accents. People walking by stared.

We had fun. We praised God. (I whispered a personal thanks for His idea of cooking teams.)

Then the Lord allowed us to do it all over again. It seemed like we'd been given the privilege to praise Him in some of the most beautiful places that He created- on towering mountaintops and by majestic forests. Now our cooking teams were about to head to deep, sparkling waters, encircled by seemingly endless tiers of mountains and forests. In the past I may have gasped over good ideas, but on the lakes in the interior of British Columbia, the only thing worthy of a gasp was the Lord and the beauty of His creation.

We found ourselves enjoying a house boating vacation on the Shushwap Lakes near Kelowna, British Columbia, not far from where we'd launched our first cooking teams a few years earlier. This time we were at a lower altitude and a much higher temperature. Once again, new teams were assembled with children who were so much more experienced in the kitchen. From the galley of our vessel came glorious meals with culinary flair and with a subtle hint of competitivemess. Oops, I mean competitiveness. I recall the night of one burnt salmon, and two frustrated cooks! We certainly had a bit of a mess.

The Lord gently showed us in His unique way how He's not just in the details of our lives, but He is the life in our details. He transported us to the mountaintops to stand in awe of Him. He called us to abide in Him in the shade of His lofty pine trees. He met us by the water's edge in the still evening under a canopy of millions of stars to be still and know He is God.

One more thing. I've stood on both sides of the kitchen counter. As a little girl I played the part of the obedient observer, longing to lovingly stir homemade soups and feel dough between my fingers. When I finally had the opportunity to stand on the other side of the counter, I remembered my childhood longings. I asked God to turn them into reality for our children, so we could create meals and build relationships together.

So choose for yourselves today my friend, but as for me and my kitchen, we will serve the Lord together... in His kingdom kitchen.

Oh, just one more little thing. Sometimes I get some really bad ideas. (You can be sure those are the ones that come from my brain and not from the mind of God.) Like the summer I booked us a cabin at Clear Lake. Over the phone the owner made it sound quite nice, but when we pulled up and saw it, I sat in the van sobbing with disappointment. I remember refusing to get out.

Within a few days, I stopped crying and we all began laughing at this cabin and ourselves. To fill you in on how heinous it really was would take another chapter. Let's just say, everyone was required to wear closed toed shoes at all times in the cabin. I made a rule... no touching the bedding. Most of us slept between the beach towels I had brought.

Even though I repeatedly asked our family not to sit on the sofa, against my impassioned advice, some did. I won't mention any names, but one night I saw him rub his face on the sofa. The next morning he had a swollen, red eye. Just one. That was the same morning we noticed a knife stabbed into the side of our cabin. At least it was on the outside. A few mornings later we woke up to a bear outside our door, finishing off the salmon skin Ron left on the barbeque the night before.

These are just a few things that happen when I go with my own ideas. You'd think I'd know by now to leave it up to the Lord. Literally... up.

I've mentioned salmon a few times in this chapter, so let me share Ron's irresistible salmon recipe. In honour of the Gladysz Family House Boating Trip, I'm calling it...

Buoy oh buoy Good Salmon

We are salmon fans. It's good for you and easy to prepare. Leftovers may even reappear as the garland to grace a salad of mixed greens. I love the explosion of colour it adds to a plate. We're going to start by going shopping for the nicest whole salmon fillet you can find. Then head to your favourite kitchen store and pick up a cedar plank. Need I say "food grade?" Ron suggested I mention that point. As if you'd go to the lumber-yard. Very important- the night before you'll need the plank, soak it in water. You can even soak it in the morning.

I'm not a poet, but I couldn't resist having a little fun...

Prepare this glaze,
that will set your salmon's flavours ablaze,
win you praise and many bouquets,
from friends who will gaze.

1/2 cup pure maple syrup, the real stuff
1/4 cup brown sugar
1 T. dry mustard
2 T. fresh orange juice
1 t. grated orange rind

Consider these your top five friends. Combine them well. Now let's move on to the salmon. Rinse it well, pat it dry and sprinkle it generously with freshly cracked peppercorns. Then brush the salmon with the glaze, but reserve about 1/4 cup for basting while cooking.

And now, the plank.
I'll be frank.
You can take the idea of the plank
to the bank.

Place the glazed salmon on the plank and plunk it on the upper shelf of your barbeque over high heat. It shouldn't go directly on the grill. If your barbeque doesn't have a shelf you can place a couple of bricks on the grate and lay your plank across them. There you go, instant shelf.

Close the lid and cook it for 10-12 minutes or until it's done. Your cooking time may vary a bit. Ron, our barbeque king, says you'll know it's done when the flesh turns from translucent to opaque.

Remember to baste the fish a few times during the cooking process.

We like to serve cedar plank salmon with sides such as smoky baked beans, Asian broccoli slaw, balsamic barbequed vegetable kabobs, Don't Mess with Texas Creamed Corn (see Chapter 12), or No Joke Artichoke and Spinach Dip (see Chapter 19).

Buoy oh buoy, this is a good salmon recipe. Every blessing You pour out I'll turn back to praise.

Fifteen

CMmmQ

**Proverbs 18:22 He who finds a wife
finds a good thing
And obtains favor from the LORD.**

Swaddled in the warmth of a handmade quilt on an indescribably cold night in early January, I fondly reflected on the recent wonderful Christmas memories the Lord had lovingly wrapped and presented to our family.

The children had now safely traveled back to their homes, and the Christmas decorations were nestled all snug in their boxes. Enveloped in my blanket, I pondered the coming year. And then God moved. All of a sudden I could feel my eyes widen, I gasped a great big gasp and the words poured from my mouth, "I have an idea!" Yes, I was talking to myself. Ron was nowhere to be seen.

The next morning, after the Lord and I had gone over some details of this idea, I approached Ron as he relaxed with his big cup of coffee. Poor man, he was in for one of my *"I have an idea"* moments.

I began to share. Sometimes I burst with enthusiasm when I explain an idea, and other times I unfold it gently and slowly. It depends. This time I felt the need to unpack things carefully, mostly because it involved Ron's 100% participation. I know these things about my husband after 30 years of marriage. As I presented my case, I could see his keen interest in the idea, which fueled my enthusiasm. I was crazy about the new idea and as you can imagine, I was delighted when he was on board.

Ron and I know two young men of God, hundreds of miles away, who are dating our precious daughters. In an effort to get to know them (the men, not the girls!) better and build a relationship with each of them, the Lord propelled us to establish CMmmQ.

At first glance it looks a lot like MMMM, from Chapter 2, and I'll admit there are some definite similarities. It's an e-mail, sent on Monday mornings, but not to our children. It's sent to the two men who are dating our cherished daughters. CMmmQ is **C**hris and **M**ichael's **M**onday **M**orning **Q**uestion. It comes from Ron each Monday morning. With a grin on his face and a glimmer in his eye he hits the send button.

We believed God for His perfect timing- the start of a new year, the start of a new adventure. What an utter surprise it must have been to these unsuspecting young men when they opened their e-mails on that Monday morning in January and read about their new weekly task.

I'm so thankful my husband keeps both his eyes on the *man* in ro*man*tic when young men take an interest in any of our daughters. Ron, a wise man and loving father, clearly outlined the details of CMmmQ to the men. He began by explaining that our home thrives on creativity (something these men already knew). He went on to say that on Monday mornings they'd each receive the same e-mail question and would have a week to respond with brief answers.

He said the purpose of CMmmQ was to stimulate their thinking and for Ron to get to know them better. Ron added that there'd be a mixture of serious topics and other questions that would make them all laugh. That must've calmed Chris and Michael's spirits. Before he unveiled the first question, he informed them that we had a special prayer time on Friday mornings and invited them to share prayer requests with us as well.

And then came the first question in bold print.

What is the first thing that attracted you to our daughter?

He thanked them and signed his name. What an adrenaline rush it was for me to see Ron hit the send button. I smiled.

I could barely contain myself. I checked our e-mail daily. Finally the first response came and we were ecstatic. Well, I'll admit I was the ecstatic one. Ron was eager to see why these men were interested in our treasured daughters. We were very pleased with their prompt, honest and candid responses. There was a comment from one of the men that really struck us. He had written,

"Thanks for your obvious commitment to my relationship with your daughter and helping us in any way to make it proceed in a positive direction." Ahhh....

Thank you Jesus. We were on a roll. These men had grasped the concept and we were delighted. Christ had already blessed us through their first answer and we praised God for bringing such God-fearing men of integrity into our girls' lives.

As I type this today, January 29th, 2009, CMmmQ is only three weeks old and our young suitors are responding weekly. The girls haven't mentioned anything to us, but at some point I'm expecting a call from them that may sound something like this, "Mom, what are you and dad up to? Why are you harassing my boyfriend? Did dad have to do this when he dated you?"

Since Ron and I don't see these young couples interact on a daily basis, we know this is a creative way to stimulate conversations and some intentional get-to-know-you dialogue. CMmmQ gives us the opportunity to pose carefully worded questions and offers our gentlemen-callers ample time to consider their responses. Throughout the week we prayerfully look to the Lord for each question and we have great fun on Sunday evenings together putting the final touches on the Monday morning e-mail. And look at what the Lord does. Even the time Ron and I spend discussing possible questions and topics for the men have turned out to be a benefit in our relationship as well. What a gift that is to us! God is good. I love Jesus.

You can be sure that as long as these outstanding young men are pursuing our daughters,

Ron will be pursuing them with CMmmQ and with regular visits across the miles for his well known early morning breakfast dates with them. I'm the contented mother who cheerfully observes all this pursuing going on, acknowledging that God is always at work around us.

But, dear friend, do you realize that you too, are being pursued? Jesus pursues each one of us because He loves us. That's always been His plan, His great idea. His plan to pursue you and me has existed from the beginning of time. No questions asked.

CMmmQ update: If you've been wondering what types of questions we've asked over the months, here's a little sample:

- Let's pretend you were given $2,000 to put towards a missions trip. Where would you go and what would you do?
- How would your parents describe you, using only three words?
- What is your favourite thing to do together as a couple?
- How do you respond when your girlfriend cries for no apparent reason?
- How would you describe your girlfriend using only three words that begin with the letter R? (R was for Ron)
- You are at a gathering with your girlfriend and it's your turn to play the game. Which would you rather do? A. Spit a live gold fish as far across the room as possible. B.

Yodel for 2 minutes. C. Play the accordion for 3 minutes. D. Guess the weight of your girlfriend.
- What could you repair most easily? A. An old deck. B. A leaky faucet. C. A fan belt. D. A broken nose.
- You've been asked to teach a Sunday school class for the summer to 3-5 year olds. Which Old Testament character would you choose and why?

A final note. Chris, the boyfriend has recently become Chris, the husband!

Sixteen

The Heart of the Platter
And Soothing Smoothies

**Psalm 92:1 & 2 It is good to give thanks to
the LORD and to sing praises to Your name,
O Most High;
To declare Your lovingkindness
in the morning
And Your faithfulness by night...**

The Heart of the Platter

You're a good mom.

You know it's been proven that breakfast is the most important meal of the day. You're aware that children who eat breakfast do better in school, have decreased hyperactivity, plus improved academic performance and behavior. You've read that breakfast aids in weight management, fuels the body and helps to provide energy for the day. You try to get breakfast into your children every morning, right? But it doesn't seem to always work.

They say they're running late, not interested, don't have time and even dare to say there's nothing good to eat in the house. And then there's this one too. They tell us they can't eat that early in the morning. We've heard it all.

Because I eat breakfast and couldn't imagine going without, I can't see how a youngster or teenager can get through the morning on an empty stomach. The Lord gave me *a (gasp) I have an idea!* moment in my quest to find a way to get my little humans to eat breakfast, After all, morning was all His idea. In Psalm 30:5 we read that a shout of joy comes in the morning. Scripture says we are to lay our prayers before Him in the morning. Sunrise, Easter morning, Christmas morning, it's all over Scripture. I think you'll agree with me that His Glory Morning Muffins are His idea too? But more on that later.

One morning as Brooklynne was busy blow-drying her hair, I stood sleepily in the kitchen, looking at the time and realizing she was once again running out of time for any sort of breakfast. It was then, in my drowsy state that the Lord gave rise to the idea of The Platter.

Suddenly I woke up. That was it! I opened the refrigerator and reached for a hard-boiled egg, some cheese and a few strawberries. After pouring a quick glass of orange juice, I grabbed a blueberry muffin and a colourful serviette. I quickly arranged it all on one of those trendy white rectangular plates. Hello little platter, you're so cute you should be on the food channel this morning! I could hear the humming of her hair drier as I knocked on the door and announced in an unusually lively voice, "Breakfast!"

Silence. And then I was invited in. Ta-da! Only by the grace of God could I have gone from a groggy state of existence to a culinary prima donna in five minutes! With a smile, she scanned the miniature banquet as I introduced her to The Platter. I took the liberty of sitting on her bed, (Girls, I'd just delivered unsolicited room service- a healthy, easy to eat, attractive breakfast) awaiting any possible kudos. She thanked me and then much to my delight, began to chatter about school and friends and life. Brooklynne talked, I listened. Then in a flurry she was out the door with a hug and a thank you. I found myself back in the kitchen praising the Lord for an empty platter and a full heart.

You see my friends, I'd served her what I thought would be a cute little breakfast platter to get her through the morning, but the Lord had a much bigger and better idea in mind. God took my offering of a few breakfast goodies and turned it into a portion of love overflowing with Himself.

I was thrilled with this idea and Brooklynne became a big fan of this morning ritual known to us as The Platter. I cherished our platter times together especially as I could see the pages of my calendar move closer to September and her departure date for Bible school 3,200 kilometers away from home. Away from breakfast platters and away from our chats. Morning platters became an opportunity for talking time (you remember talking time?) and then matured into The Evening Platter, which helped to get her through homework and studying. She'd take a break, we'd have a little visit, and then I'd disappear with an empty platter. I'm smiling even today as I type this.

She made her exit from Saskatchewan that September. I missed our platter times, but you can guess one of the first things I served her when she came home for Christmas. Hmm... perhaps on our next visit to Texas, I could ask Sheila, the cook at Bible school, if I could putter around her kitchen for a few minutes one morning or at bedtime.

So girlfriend, I to urge you to take on The Platter, a precious little number. But if you find yourself running out the door in the mornings before your children are awake, don't dismay, perhaps try to adopt the evening platter idea if that works better in your life. Remember, what works in our home will look different in your home.

I'm convinced that evening platters can help your high schooler get through the last bit of homework. It'll improve their grades and love of learning. Okay, I'm exaggerating a wee bit, but platters have taken up residence in our home and are here to stay. I'll venture to say I believe they can work well somewhere in yours too. I really do.

As for the treasures on the platter, I'd choose food with a variety of colours and textures on a plate- muffins, pecans, almonds, dried fruit, fresh fruit, carrot sticks, cucumber slices, a hard boiled egg, a couple of different kinds of cheeses and crackers. Another popular choice was a simple cheese melt with freshly ground pepper, garnished with a few apples slices. (A cheese melt is simply some cheese melted on bread under the broiler for a few minutes.) Multi-grain tortilla chips and salsa. Sí, amiga!

The best part for me was always when I knocked on the bedroom door, I was not only announcing snack time, I was bringing a blessing to her from the Lord. I could see my child sigh in relief, knowing she had a breakfast set before her that she could nibble on as she finished getting ready for school. Or in the evening, smiling as she realized it was time to take a well-earned break from her books. As we talked about life for those few precious minutes, I was always thankful for God's goodness to us as a family, and for these special times.

Soothing Smoothies

So now you know that The Platter was a huge hit in our home over the past few years, but if the platter idea isn't working for you, don't be discouraged, here's another idea that might smooth things out for you. Nothing soothes like a smoothie.

> *I just read that little paragraph to Ron and he casually nodded. I really wanted him to say he loved the creative flair and play on words, blah blah blah. All he did was nod. He was watching the fishing channel on television. Bad timing on my part. But, let's be honest, I was really looking for some praise. Just a little, from my man who has encouraged me through this project. But all I got was a nod. Did I mention that yet?*

> *I headed off to bed and couldn't sleep. God was up to something. Remember He doesn't sleep when we do, so He's available to speak when-ever He wants. His point? If this is really God's*

book, then He's the Author of anything good in it, including that paragraph. So again I see who gets the praise. Settle down Stephanie and stop getting your desires in the way of the Lord's. It's a reminder that God's ideas are divine and my ideas are all fleshy. Hmm... I hadn't planned this devotional detour in the chapter, but God sure had. Let's get back to the business of smoothies now.

Feeling hot and sweaty after working in the yard? Have a smoothie. Need a mid morning pick me up to get you through until lunch? Make yourself and anyone else around you a smoothie. Do you have hungry children bursting through your door at 3:30 p.m. each day? Blend up some smoothies and serve them with cookies as an after school snack. Is it late in the evening and you know the children will need a treat? A refreshing smoothie is the thing. Remember you're not just serving a yummy nutritious beverage, you're nurturing relationships.

Every time I made a smoothie, I smiled because I knew I'd have a few minutes with my child. Rarely was my smoothie offer declined. If you're feeling ambitious, you can always offer the ultimate.... "Who wants a platter *and* a smoothie?" Girls, it's my heart's cry for God to use me in small ways to bless our children and their friends in our home. Inevitably, when it was smoothie time, the boys who were in the basement grinding out university papers and the girls who were upstairs doing homework, would emerge and we'd all find ourselves gathered around the kitchen table together.

A tall refreshing smoothie invigorates and soothes. It looks like golden sunshine in a glass and smells like a tropical vacation at the beach. It's a good idea in the morning and evening. And as for me and my house, we will serve the Lord… and smoothies. I really like that picture and Scripture, so that's why I've used it twice already. I hope that's okay.

From Brooklynne's Blender

I asked Brooklynne the smoothie-lover in our home for a contribution to this section. So from her blender to yours, these are her top picks, happy blending.…

raspberries, strawberries or peaches, preferably fresh, but frozen is also good
vanilla yogurt, or plain yogurt with a touch of honey
orange juice

You can have some fun adjusting the amounts of these delightful ingredients to suit your taste buds of the day.

Peachy Keen Smoothie

1 cup skim milk
2 cups yogurt, choose your favourite flavour
1 cup orange juice
2 cups peeled and roughly chopped fresh peaches

Pour milk, yogurt and orange juice into blender, and then toss in the peaches. Blend on medium for 30 seconds. Blend again if needed. Pour into a glass, pop in a straw, find a good friend and sip slowly on a porch swing, barefooted and wearing a comfy sundress.

Tropical Vacation in a Glass... looks like a piña colada, smells like a piña colada, tastes like a piña colada

2 1/2 cups pineapple juice
1/2 cup plain yogurt
1 frozen banana
1 cup pineapple chunks, fresh or frozen (fresh is much better)
a splash of flaked coconut

Pour juice and yogurt into blender. Top with banana, pineapple and coconut. Blend on medium for 30 seconds. Peek in. Blend again if needed. Pour into colourful glasses and dream of the beach.

Basically Smooth Smoothie

1 cup orange juice
1 cup plain yogurt
1 cup strawberries

This basic smoothie recipe can be altered to suit your family's taste. Substitute berry blends, yogurt types and fruit in season or from your freezer. Go ahead: create your own signature smoothie! I keep some protein powder on hand and will often add a 1/4 cup as a booster. And remember, a shot of chocolate syrup turns a breakfast smoothie into a dessert faster then you can say soothing smoothie.

We love raspberries (you'll need to add a touch of honey), mango, fresh oranges, blueberries and watermelon. Vanilla yogurt is tasty, but I often use strawberry or field berry. There are many new varieties of berry juices in the grocery store, so you may want to experiment with the pomegranate, berry and apple blends. Give them a chance, they won't let you down.

Muffins are a great addition to a morning platter. These muffins are glorious. They almost deserve one minute of silence.

His Glory Morning Muffins

1 cup whole wheat flour
1/2 cup all purpose flour
1 cup regular oats
1 T. cinnamon
3/4 cup brown sugar (or a wee bit more if you like 'em sweeter)
2 t. baking soda
1/4 t. salt
1 cup plain yogurt
1 cup mashed bananas (about 3 ripe bananas)
1 egg
1 cup shredded carrots
3/4 cup chopped apricots
1/2 cup fancy flaked coconut, the long kind
1/2 cup chopped walnuts

Pre-heat your oven to 350° F. and prepare 12 muffin cups. Combine flours, oats, cinnamon, sugar, soda and salt in a large bowl. In a separate bowl combine yogurt, banana and egg. Add to dry ingredients. Gently fold in carrots, apricots, coconut and nuts. Spoon batter into muffin cups and bake for 15-18 minutes or until muffin springs back when touched lightly. Cool on racks. Enjoy hot and fresh, or freeze for a future platter. To God be the glory, great things He hath done....

Seventeen

Cleaned up, Signed up and Served up

1 Peter 4:9 & 10 Be hospitable to one another without complaint. As each one has received a special gift, employ it in serving one another as good stewards of the manifold grace of God.

Cleaned up

One brilliant December morning a number of years ago I realized the strangest thing.

I was in full swing decorating, baking and cleaning in my usual pre-Christmas way. The carols rang out from the family room. I went about my work happily, watching the cookies in the oven and scratching things off my list that was as long as Santa's. I added to-do things to the list that I had just done so I could experience the thrill of marking them off. (Don't tell me you've never done that before.)

Outside my window the subzero temperature with life threatening wind chill factors were of no concern to me. The scent of household cleaner that filled the air only served to exhilarate me more as I whizzed through the house.

As one who commonly talks to myself, today I spoke not a word but went straight to my work. I recall thinking "what next" as I zipped from one glorious task to another. From room to room I soared, smiling contentedly as each room gleamed back at me with thanks. I gazed around the family room, the most festive looking of all... the stockings were hung by the chimney with care and as I sprang through the house, visions of sugarplums danced in my head. With one quick glance of approval on the main floor, up the staircase I rose.

My attention turned to one room in particular that needed some extra special pampering before I could consider everything ready for the Christmas holidays. It was a room I'd sat in many times over the past months whenever I needed a quiet place to abide and pray. On that day, at that moment, in that bedroom I paused one more time to thank God for His faithfulness. Then I set to work knowing this still, vacant room would soon house the precious subject of many of my prayers. In seven hours Genevieve was coming home from college for Christmas.

You see my friends, when the first one of our little flock left home it was weird and wonderful, at the same time. The thought of her coming home made me tingle.

This is the strange thing. I found myself scrubbing our home from top to bottom, arranging and rearranging, cooking favourite recipes, dusting things that didn't need dusting, making sure that absolutely everything was in its place. Normally when I was preparing for houseguests, I would've had Genevieve helping with the to do list. Now it was all for her! I'll admit sometimes I'm a bit over the top.

Almost instinctively I knew her bedroom had to be transformed into the most welcoming room in the whole house. I wanted it to be a reflection of everything that was pounding in my heart, "I love you baby, I'm thrilled beyond belief that you're home for Christmas and this will always be your home to come home to." Have I mentioned that occasionally I can be a bit over the top?

I couldn't think of anything better to do that day than turn an average bedroom into a haven that screamed, "welcome home" for our daughter. The ideas in my mind were endless. A pink poinsettia or a mini-evergreen plant? A bowl of Christmas candy or dark chocolate? Or both? The latest magazine featuring Christmas baking or make-ahead appetizers? A basket of Christmas oranges? Definitely a pair of new warm socks and an extra fluffy fleece blanket. A love note under her pillow or in the top drawer? Scented tea lights or a pine candle? New flannel pajamas or a cozy robe? Extra hangers in the closet and lots of room for suitcases. A little collection of framed family pictures brimming with memories of past Christmases. In the end I couldn't decide which idea to go with, so I think I went with all of the above.

The idea suddenly hit me that I was doing exactly what God has commanded in His Word.

This was a unique way to be hospitable, within our home, to one of our own. And God caused me to fulfill His will with such joy! What better place to teach hospitality to the children but in our home? What an idea- show hospitality to one another in the family and then take the lessons we've learned and extend them to our neighbours and friends. As mothers, if we demonstrate hospitality in the name of Jesus to our children, we're helping to equip them to be hospitable to the *one anothers* in their world. Hospitality grows up at home. That makes me smile.

Signed up

I love the idea of making guests in our home feel as special as they really are to us. Our front entry is a very spacious area. It's large enough for a bench that my father built, an oversized mirror, a floor vase of flowers, an antique cabinet with some cupboards (which has served as a lost-and-found for years), and dozens of pairs of shoes. As previously mentioned, we've often had a lot of people in our home at any given time. You recall Chapter 10?

Honestly though, that's the way we like it and we've always treasured having so many dear friends of all ages in our home over the decades. One day I got the idea to add something to this roomy entry that would help create a more welcoming atmosphere for guests.

It happened while we were on vacation at the lake. The girls and I were doing a little bit of the girl thing we like to do, when I came across the best idea of the summer. (Shopping can be a time of divine inspiration to those who are truly willing to be open.) Remember, great ideas can pop up anywhere, anytime. We were in an adorable little gift store when I had a *(gasp) I have an idea!* moment. I've learned there are times I need to exercise self-control when I'm struck with a new idea. And being in a delicate gift store, I knew this was one of those times. I gasped a series of tiny gasps as I gestured towards the girls and clutched my idea in the palms of my hands. I'd found a guest book.

I was elated. My mind went fast forward. I pictured our friends gathered in the front entry, signing the guest book as they headed out the door. I imagined Ron and me reading their comments and thanking God for joyous times with friends in our home. Ahh... bliss.

Suddenly I was jolted back to reality as I heard the girls casually remark something like, "oh that's nice, are you going to buy it?" They must not have understood this was a big idea moment in my life. We were about to begin some serious guest booking.

Hence, there's a guest book that lives at the front door, on top of the cabinet at just the right height for writing a quick note and leaving a permanent record of good times in our home. We've now completed our first book and recently I came upon another... on sale thank you very much. We've begun volume two. As we look back through the pages of each book, we nod, recalling special times and people God brought to our home. Our guest books are like a diary of God's blessings of friendships. A blessing from His heavenly home to our earthly home.

Guest books are a good idea. Sign up.

Served up

Here come the brides.

During a 10-month period several years ago, we received 11 wedding invitations and also attended many, many bridal showers. These events seemed to become a weekly ritual. Our daughters and I even hosted several showers and a bachelorette party in our home. It was a pretty girly time around the house. In one of the empty bedrooms I had numerous wedding and shower gifts lined up as if they were awaiting their debut on the worldwide wedding stage.

Alexandra always tells me to shop for brides from their gift registries, but I just never have because the Lord seems to give me other ideas. And during this busy wedding season in our lives, He reminded me about our guest books. I gasped. What a great idea. The first one I purchased was for Lindsay and Jill, a beautiful young couple. He's a professional golfer and she's a teacher. I was delighted when I heard they loved the book that now lives in their Vancouver home. I wonder if there are any names of famous golfers in that book? Hmm... more importantly, I pray that their names are written in the Master's Book. And I don't mean in Augusta.

Another year, another wedding. Genevieve was maid of honour for her friend, Sheena. I mentioned her to you before. I needed a gift to show Sheena how much we loved her. I knew she and Jeremy were a young couple that would create a Christ-centered, hospitable and loving home. They needed a guest book! But this time the Lord also suggested I add another element of Himself to the gift.

God took me to the Old Testament, to the book of Joshua, the sixth book of the Bible. These bold words are given to us in Joshua 24:15, "... but as for me and my house, we will serve the LORD." That verse is engraved on the brass door knocker on our front door. I wanted to add that same symbol of a home for Christ to the gift I was preparing for Jeremy and Sheena.

I made a quick trip to the hardware store and engraving shop. Several days later I had the Word of God permanently engraved on brass, declaring that behind the door of this soon-to-be-home, the Lord God Almighty was worshiped and served. Guests in Jeremy and Sheena's home would be greeted by the Word of the Lord on one side of the door and by a young couple who loved Jesus on the other side of the door.

I want to show our guests that we cherish our friendships and times of fellowship. A door knocker stating this home is for Christ can be one of the many little steps in welcoming your guests in the name of Jesus. An inviting guest book tells them you're thankful for time together. I'm humbled to have learned that God can use our home to express hospitality. Best idea ever.

Oh, a few more things... honestly girlfriends, I absolutely love sharing ideas with you, so here are a few more ideas to consider. If this whole guest book idea moves you, keep your eyes open for some unique ones- they're out there and you'll come across some charming ones, but they can be hard to find. I gave Genevieve one when she set up her first little home in Texas at His Hill Bible School where she serves. She's had hundreds of students through her door, and many have written what seem like short stories in her guest book. For her, it's a fond look back at the friends God has brought to her school and into her home. She's now on volume two.

Last week our daughter Alexandra "got a fiancé," as she puts it. She got engaged to Chris, the fine young man of God I told you about in Chapter 15, CMmmQ. I'll soon be visiting the cutest store I know to find them the perfect guest book for their home. Then I'll need to find a shiny brass door knocker.

One more thing. Guest books are easy to package and mail. I like that. You will too. When you find one you like, why not buy a few and tuck them away in a special place for future gift giving? Try to remember where that special place is. At times I've had issues in this area.

Last thing. During the Christmas season, I keep my eyes open for extra-special items such as ornaments, table linens, sparkly décor, candles, wreaths and cookbooks. I keep them tucked away. As invitations arrive in my mailbox, I wrap up a variety of these goodies and give them as shower and wedding gifts. Most young couples have said it's great to receive Christmas decorations as gifts because they have a start on making their home festive for the holidays.

Recipe time again!

Speaking of bridal showers, here's a happy recipe that's sure to bring on applause and cheers. Copy the recipe onto a pretty card and include it with your gift to the bride. She'll be thankful for a no fuss appetizer. Her guests will gush. She will shine.

Wait for it! Pepper Cheese Dip

I call this "wait for it" because it takes a few minutes for the zip of this dip to kick in! Mmm....

8 oz. cream cheese
2 T. freshly cracked black pepper
1 T. finely chopped fresh garlic
1 t. chopped fresh dill
1 T. chopped fresh parsley
1 t. finely chopped chives
a pinch of dried tarragon, basil, marjoram

(If you don't have all these dried spices, you can cheat a bit and life will go on. The key ingredients are pepper, garlic, dill and parsley.)

Bring the cream cheese to room temperature. Here's the easy part. Blend everything together by hand or in a food processor until all the ingredients are really good friends. Pack the cheese into an attractive bowl and chill it all day. Wait for it! An hour or so before serving take it out of the refrigerator and admire it. Serve it with some crackers and oh sister, you're on a cheese dip pleasure trip.

If there's any left, it'll keep in the refrigerator for about a week. Ron puts this cheese blend into scrambled eggs. Brilliant!

Eighteen

And the Winner is...

Colossians 3:21 Fathers, do not exasperate your children, so that they will not lose heart.

A t times I become exasperated and lose heart when I'm in the grocery store.

This often happens while I'm happily sniffing pineapples or quietly cheering for plump, ripe raspberries in the dead of winter. This may not make any sense to you, but it sure doesn't make any sense to me when I hear parents screaming at their children in the produce department.

Fathers and mothers, do not exasperate your children, so that they will not lose heart.

I know. I understand. I've taken our four children, who are less than seven years apart in age, to the grocery store. Many times. It's not easy. It's not always pretty, but neither is a raging adult.

Fathers and mothers, please do not exasperate your children, so that they will not lose heart.

Ladies, cherish your children, even during those tense and intense trips to the grocery store with them. Here's why. All that nutritious food you buy at the grocery store causes them to grow up, then they move out, leaving you at home with no one bursting through the door at 3:30 p.m. for hot chocolate and cookies, or to tuck in at night. Re-read Chapter 11.

I did some research on the words "exasperate" and "lose heart" using a dictionary and a variety of Bible translations.

Some Bible versions replaced the word exasperate with embitter, aggravate, nag and most commonly, provoke. Let that sink in for a minute. God is commanding us not to do those things to our children. Then I examined the words, lose heart. I found that many Bible translations used the word discourage. Hmm... why would we want to discourage our children? Some dictionary synonyms for discourage are- crush, dash and demoralize. These are sad words.

The opposite of exasperate is- calm, comfort, ease, please, soothe, encourage, inspire and spur on. The opposite of lose heart is- inspire, hearten, encourage, cheer, brighten, reassure, strengthen, refresh and restore. Do you know children or teenagers who need some comforting? Or some inspiration, or maybe a little encouragement? That's all I'll say. Perhaps you can go over those thoughts with the Lord in your quiet time.

And the winner is... this idea started with a brochure we found on board the houseboat we'd rented one summer a few years ago. (You may recall some good cooking stories from Chapter 14.) In this boating safety pamphlet was an outline of the phonetic alphabet used by boaters, aviators, the military and police. We wondered if the houseboat rental office back on shore really expected us prairie folk to have radio communication with them using this foreign language.

However, at some misty point on our voyage, the idea popped into my head that as a sea-faring family for seven glorious days, navigating the spectacular waters of British Columbia's interior, we'd have to learn this new alphabet. Just for some fun. To encourage, refresh, inspire, strengthen and cheer.

At first, some of the crew members were hesitant to get into this game, but it wasn't long before everyone was on board (ha!) with this whimsical idea. Each evening, snug in our galley, we'd practice memorizing the alphabet bit by bit. We had some good laughs along the way, but by the end of the week everyone had mastered this new language. The vacation ended and everyone thought that was pretty much the end of the phonetic alphabet world. Hmm....

For some reason, I kept the little scrap from the boating brochure that outlined the odd alphabet. Throwing it out was like tossing the memories of our trip overboard. Alpha Bravo Charlie found its way onto the refrigerator and made me smile each time I looked at it, recalling how much fun we'd had on holidays. How we'd all gotten ridiculously competitive as we raced to recite the alphabet.

It was that one word, competitive, that set things off in my head, I gasped and yelled out loud to myself in the kitchen, "I have an idea." I was at the computer in an instant, composing an e-mail to the children as fast as I could. See Stephanie type. See Stephanie smile.

Friends, despite all this silliness, my very serious intent is always to build relationships, draw us closer together and to inject some playfulness into the family. To brighten the children's hearts, not to belittle them. To inspire, not to exasperate. And the Lord was about to give me the desires of my heart. (I also wanted to find out who still remembered the phonetic alphabet.)

The new idea was a Sibling E-mail Contest. It had a few guidelines and one great prize for the winner. In my e-mail, I outlined the contest rules. It read...

- The phonetic alphabet contest is open to all Gladysz children.
- The entrants must phone home at 9:00 p.m. in three days.
- The first caller will have the opportunity to correctly recite by memory, the phonetic alphabet to me. If he or she is correct, they will be declared the winner.
- If he or she is incorrect, I will take the next caller and repeat the process.
- My decision of a winner is final and non-negotiable.

That was about it. I clearly remember the excitement that swelled in me as I hit the send button that day. It's the simple things of life I enjoy most- like having some good fun with our children. To refresh and build up, not to discourage. But now I had to wait three days to see what kind of response I'd get, if any at all.

The next day things got started. The first response was a hilarious reply from Alexandra who was a first year college student in Calgary at the time. In a very business-like tone she stated in her e-mail that she was "consumed with research papers, group assignments and mid-term exams and wouldn't be able to participate in the contest because she had real work to do." One down, three to go, but I was still convinced this was a really good idea that had great possibilities.

Three long days later, just before 9:00 p.m. I slipped upstairs to our bedroom and sat by the phone like a teenage girl waiting and wondering if her crush would call. At 9:00 p.m. sharp my heart leapt with joy as the phone rang. It was Jamison calling from his room in the basement, thrilled to be the first caller. He was raised on a hockey rink, so he loves a little competition. But seconds before he began to give his answer, I got a beep and heard Genevieve, our yellow rose of Texas on the other line. She too, has an "ambitious" side in her after all those years as a competitive figure skater. I put her on hold.

Now we had a real contest going on. I let Jamison begin... Alpha, Beta, Charlie, Delta, Echo, Foxtrot... ahh... I knew he'd made an error, but I let him continue through the alphabet. I thanked him for participating and working hard to learn the alphabet, but informed him of his error. (It's Bravo, not Beta.) I moved on to Genevieve's call, she did her thing and got it right. She cheered, I

161

chuckled over the whole thing and then I think she gave her brother a quick call so they could share a good laugh together over their mother's crazy ideas. Exactly as I had planned it should be.

That night I went to bed with a smile on my face and a happy, happy heart. We'd all had some fun, interacted with each other in a lively way and made some great memories. I can say that with confidence, because today, five years later, I called Genevieve to ask her what details she remembered about that first contest and she was able to give me a play by play accurate recap of the entire night. I could sense a hint of competitiveness in her sweet voice over the phone as she relived the episode. She even recalled being at her friend Jody's house when she made the call and that her prize was a Switchfoot CD. Does anyone venture to say that some day this young woman will be running a few contests of her own as a mom?

In the role that God has assigned me as a mother, I see how I'm called to foster inspiration, not exasperation in our children's lives. I want to embrace, not embarrass, and to encourage instead of embitter. You may not find these contests outlined anywhere in the job description of a parent, but for us it's been a great way to connect the family dots all over North America.

Will you seek the Lord, dear one, to discover what He'll work out for you? Remember it won't look the same for your family. I'm here for God to use me to inspire you to look to Him for His will in your family.

We had so much fun with that first contest; I knew there'd be more to come. And there has been. Now, I don't want to tell you about too many of our contest ideas, in order to allow you freedom to be creative as God directs you. But I'll give you a little peek at a few more ideas God gave me.

There was the squirrel contest. We had a family of quirky squirrels living in our backyard because I'd been feeding them (unsalted) peanuts for many months. These bold little creatures were the most precious things I'd ever seen, until they literally moved into our attic. At that point, and thousands of dollars later, Ron announced that I'd never be allowed to feed another squirrel. Ever. I agreed but that didn't stop me from one day declaring, *"(gasp) I have an idea!"* Suddenly squirrels became the topic of a brand new customized contest.

Even as I type this I find myself smiling over what was a spirited contest. Before I'd put together the plans for the contest I knew exactly what the unique prize would be for the lucky winner. For reasons I couldn't disclose in the rules, only Gladysz girls were eligible to enter. This time entrants were required to submit a short essay, as creative as possible, about squirrels. That was it. And once again, Alexandra announced she had more important university assignments to work on than a squirrel essay. That still makes me laugh as I picture her reading my e-mail, shaking her head and telling Lyn, her roommate, that her mother had lost her mind for sure this time. Perhaps she may have even used the word "nuts." (Ha!)

I was elated when I found two lengthy squirrel essays greeting me in my inbox a week later. Both Genevieve and Brooklynne had spent considerable time researching habits and interesting facts about squirrels. Those girls of mine. I had two very well-written, factual and creative pieces before me. One of the girls had even named her squirrel! Now what was I to do? How could I judge which one was better? They were both great.

In the end I was able to present both Genevieve and Brooklynne with a reward. I went deep into our basement and located a very special old suitcase I had tucked away.

The prizes were antique treasures that had been in the family for three generations. Two luxurious heirloom squirrel fur stoles. Picture a mink stole, but in squirrel. (I'm laughing so hard right now.) Why would my family own two squirrel stoles? My dear mother tells me they were a very popular item when she was a teenager in the 1940's. Hmm... I don't need to tell you I quickly discovered squirrel stoles are not so popular with young women of today.

I can't describe the girls' reactions when they opened the gift bags stuffed with their very own squirrel stoles. Let's just say I recently took them to a man who buys furs to make stuffed animals. Can you believe my girls didn't want them? I could see Genevieve's point since she was living in Texas, but Brooklynne was living in Saskatchewan at the time.

And then there was the Family Trivia Contest, which consisted of a number of questions regarding dates, ages, times and places of different family events. It involved some math and asking each other a few questions. This was an easy, fun and interactive contest. Again, Genevieve and Brooklynne went head-to-head on this one for a gift card to their favourite clothing store.

A couple more ideas. A few months ago I ran Mom's Favourite Smells Contest in which the children had to submit a list of my favourite scents. Hilarious. This week I sent out Dad's Favourite Places to Hang Out Contest. Our children know us well and have a healthy sense of humour.

God is great. We all know that. His ideas and plans for us are perfect and let's remember He calls us to spur one another on. That's all I've ever intended in these playful contests. Keeping it lively and alive in Christ. No, you won't find a direct Scripture reference that talks about family contests. And yes, there are many more "spiritual" ways of fulfilling the command in Colossians not to exasperate our children. I pray you will seek God to reveal those to you.

Now it's your turn. What will you do to calm, and not condemn your children? How will you cheer your child on in the name of the Lord? As I think of the best way to end this chapter, I can only go back to the Words of the Lord God Almighty who says it best in Colossians. "Fathers, do not exasperate your children so that they will not lose heart." Mothers too.

Meanwhile back in the grocery store, I'm still ogling over fresh pineapple and raspberries. This brown velvety recipe for a chocolate mousse loaf came to mind and I have to share it with you. I rejoice over the gift of chocolate as I make and serve this... consider this pure joy my sister!

Chocolicious Joy

2 cups whipping cream
3 egg yolks
16 oz. semisweet chocolate
1/2 cup butter
1/2 cup corn syrup
1/4 cup icing sugar
1 t. pure vanilla

Sassy Raspberry Sauce

1 1/2 cups fresh raspberries
1/4 cup corn syrup
1 cup fresh pineapple cut into small chunks

Combine 1/2 cup of the whipping cream with the egg yolks in a bowl until the two have fallen totally in love. In a medium saucepan heat chocolate, butter and corn syrup over low heat just until the chocolate and butter have melted. Remove from heat and slowly stir chocolate into the egg yolk mixture. Place pan over low heat and cook until the sauce says, "I'm thick now." Remove from heat and cool. In a bowl beat remaining whipping cream, icing sugar and vanilla to form soft peaks. Lovingly fold in the chocolate mixture until thoroughly blended. Pour into a loaf pan that has been lined with plastic wrap. Don't skip that step. Refrigerate for about 8 hours or overnight. Gaze at it often and give thanks.

For the raspberry sauce, puree the raspberries in your blender. Stir in the corn syrup and chill for a few hours. To serve, invert loaf onto a rectangular serving platter, remove the plastic, drizzle with the luscious raspberry sauce and arrange pineapple chunks around the loaf. Serve immediately to 12 chocolate enthusiasts.

Mercy me, this is good.

Nineteen

Ahh... the Spa

Proverbs 31:30 Charm is deceitful and beauty is vain, But a woman who fears the LORD, she shall be praised.

As you read the title of this chapter and the corresponding Scripture, you may think I'm contradicting myself. I'm delighted if you've noticed there's a clash between the spa and the Scripture, but God led me to intentionally pair Ahh... the Spa, with Proverbs 31:30.

I'm about to write an entire chapter about the luxury of spa-ing with your daughter, but I want to preface it with the words of our Lord who clearly tells us His thoughts on outward beauty. He says that beauty is vain.

My thesaurus expands on the word vain- arrogant, conceited, egotistical, haughty, inflated, narcissistic, proud, and puffed up. Yikes sister! In contrast, one of the most stunning ways in which a godly woman can be clothed is with the fear of the Lord. Then she shall be praised.

With that vivid truth set before our powdered noses and manicured fingertips, I'll proceed cautiously. Let's remember to keep this beauty thing in check and under control. Moderation Stephanie, moderation girls.

What is it about the whole spa experience that draws us to these heavenly escapes? Could it be their polished marketing skills that invite us to recharge, renew, relieve, rejuvenate, replenish, revive, relax, retreat and refresh? Or perhaps we women simply need a brief time-out. Have you ever wished someone would say to you, "I can see by your behaviour that you need some time-out alone in your room to think about some things?" Would you then run to your room, fill the bathtub with the bubbliest bubble bath you have and soak your stress away for a few hours? Someone please send me to my room!

Throughout our child-raising years my bathroom was my spa. Going to the real spa wasn't a priority in my life. Going to the rink was. (Now there's an idea. Hockey rinks could advertise a 45-minute mini-pedicure for mothers who have to be at the arena an hour before each game. Or in between periods while the ice gets polished, our nails could get a 15-minute express polish. I'm picturing a fuchsia sign positioned between the skate sharpening booth and the stinky dressing rooms advertising... Pink Rink Spa.)

For years, my bathroom was my spa until one gorgeous June day about 10 years ago. I dropped Genevieve off at the spa for a manicure and pedicure the day before her high school graduation. As I drove away I sensed something was very wrong. Suddenly I found myself on the verge of a little gasp and a big, new, plush idea.

I told myself I should've been there with Genevieve, beside her in a white, overstuffed leather pedicure chair, exposing my tired little toes to a gifted woman who'd do her utmost to gently renovate them. I should've been sitting at the manicure counter with her sipping walnut green tea as we chatted about her graduation. Why wasn't I at the spa with her?

This may all sound very silly to you, but a decade ago I was still stuck in my bathroom with a bottle of gooey, old nail polish and a dusty, dusty-rose candle. The discovery of the spa was a luxurious new idea for me. I soon realized this could be a heavenly way to connect with my beloved daughters. Oh, thank you Jesus for making us women.

I also decided something else very important. Women should never spa alone. A girl should always pair up with another special woman in her life- girlfriend, daughter, mother, granddaughter, sister, cousin- choose someone to share the ahh... the spa moment with you. It's sad to spa alone. In my own weird sort of way, I'm passionate about this issue.

Many years have passed since that dazzling revelation occurred to me. Our three daughters have since enthusiastically bought into the spa idea. Recently, Genevieve announced that her new favourite past-time is to go spa-ing. So when Ron and I are in Texas, Genevieve and I sneak away to the spa for a few hours. Ron heads out to shoot some skeet and eat some meat.

Each time I plan a trip to Calgary to spend time with Alexandra, she asks if we can visit the spa together. This was especially common during her poor-ish student days. Brooklynne, our youngest, caught on quickly.

When our daughters and I need time together, the first idea that usually comes up is, ahh... the spa. Manicure, pedicure, massage, facial. We'll take anything- it doesn't have to be the whole day. An hour is just fine. We'll even take the 45-minute express.

Our time at the spa is only the beginning, the best is yet to come. With freshly polished toes we carefully tiptoe into a quiet restaurant for some lunch where we can easily nestle into a two-hour heart-to-heart over a salad and a fragrant pot of herbal tea. We touch on familiar topics- friends, school, ministry, relationships, decorating, rec-ipes, home making, spiritual matters and their Boaz. (More on him at the very end of this chapter.) We laugh, cry, and celebrate our relationship as mother and daughter, and daughters of the King.

Just before all the children came home one Christmas, I gasped and... you know what hap-pened. We ladies needed to have a little spa time over the holidays together! What an idea- The First Annual All Girls Christmas Homecoming Spa and Lunch Afternoon. Ron gave us his blessing and we headed to a funky new day spa here in Regina. It was the afternoon of Christmas Eve; the tem-perature was a savage -45° C. when we emerged from the spa in flip-flops. Of course our daugh-ters had to pose for a picture in the snow that would prove to their Texas friends that we are all still Canadians at heart.

We've made spa memories in Regina, Calgary, San Antonio and Denver. We have a lot of states and provinces yet to cover. But while we wait for those times to transpire, there's another way to enjoy the spa experience.

A superb alternative is the home spa. It's always great fun, allows room for lots of creativity and comes with a very attractive price tag. Ingredients for the night include relaxing music, groups of candles, good snacks and a few girls-friends or family, or a bit of both. Cocooned in tranquility, our home becomes a personal spa. I love this idea.

Take a look at *www.spaindex.com* for some incredibly easy and interesting recipes for your home spa. You'll find recipes for a blueberry toner, chocolate facial mask, apple-pear anti-wrinkle cream and papaya pumpkin facial. Now isn't this a great idea? (Remember whose ideas these really are.) Be careful to keep the spa ingredients and your finger food separate so your spa enthusiasts don't drink the blueberry toner or dip bananas into the chocolate facial. That wouldn't be proper spa etiquette.

Let's set aside all this girly fun. It's late and I should be in bed, but a *(gasp) I have an idea!* moment just came down from above. I couldn't sleep even if I tried.

So I give you... Heaven's 10 Point Spa Checklist

- If we have skin that's glowing, let's be sure our radiance is a reflection of our time spent with the Lord God Almighty.
- If we have feet that are refreshed, let's be sure to fall at the feet of Jesus each day.
- If we have a good hair day, let's be sure to wear the helmet of salvation.
- If we have the latest purse in our hand, let's be sure to praise God for the great acts He performed with His mighty hand and out-stretched arm.
- If we have our favourite perfume splashed behind our ears, let's be sure to live a life with an aroma pleasing to the Lord.
- If we have perfectly applied eye make-up, let's be sure to fix our eyes on Jesus, the author and perfecter of faith.
- If we have lips that are beautifully coloured, let's be sure to open our mouths in wisdom.
- If we are wearing the cutest little outfit as we head to the spa, let's be sure we're clothed with humility towards one another.
- If we have on our all-time favourite shoes, let's be sure we turn our feet from evil.
- If we have hands and nails with a fresh manicure, let's be sure to remember what Christ's hands, and nails mean in our lives.

Ahh... the Spa. Three good words.
Charm is deceitful. Three better words.

Beauty is vain. Three even better words.
Fear the Lord. The three best words. Amen?

Is it home spa night at your place tonight? Be sure to serve some goodies to nibble on. Here are a few scrumptious ideas from my three favourite girls.

Brooklynne would serve...

Whoop dee doo Fondue

It all begins with semi-sweet, dark or white chocolate melted with some evaporated milk. Serve this warm with chunks of angel food cake, brownies, pretzels and lots of cut up fresh fruit- bananas, apples and pineapple. Make a lemony fruit dip as an extra side treat. Oh baby. Come to me most scrumptious fondue.

Genevieve would serve...

No Joke Artichoke and Spinach Dip

8 oz. cream cheese, softened
3/4 cup sour cream
2 garlic cloves crushed
freshly ground pepper
2 T. chopped parsley and dill, fresh please
1 small jar marinated artichokes, drained and chopped

2 cups of chopped fresh spinach (fresh is so much better)
1 cup of shredded cheese, like Monterey Jack

This is easy. Stir together all the ingredients except for the cheese. It comes later. Pour the mixture into a pretty 9" ovenproof dish. Then comes the cheese. Bake this for about 25 minutes at 350° F. Soon the dip will bubble and the cheese will become lightly browned. Now it's ready to serve with Very Hip Pita Chips. This dip could very possibly be the best thing I've ever eaten. It may even put a sparkle in your eyes.

Very Hip Pita Chips

6 fresh whole wheat pitas
olive oil for brushing
dried herbs such as dill, oregano, basil, tarragon, fresh ground pepper, sea salt, paprika, cumin... I love cumin

Preheat oven to 350° F.

Cut the pitas into wedges. Brush each one with olive oil mixed with a sprinkling of dried herbs. Mmm... bake on a baking sheet until golden. Watch carefully because they can burn very quickly. I know that.

Alexandra would serve...

Baby-Blue Buttermilk Crepes

2 eggs
1 cup buttermilk
1 t. vanilla
1/2 cup sugar
1 t. cinnamon
1 1/2 cups flour
1 t. baking powder
2 T. melted butter

With great enthusiasm please whisk together the eggs, buttermilk and vanilla. Add sugar. Sift together the cinnamon, flour and baking powder. Then whisk this into the buttermilk mixture. Add melted butter. Add more buttermilk until you reach a pourable consistency. Let batter sit 10-15 minutes. That's so the bubbles calm down a bit. (Alexandra suggests the sitting time is the thing to do. I skip that step and get them right into the pan.)

Lightly grease a little crepe pan or a 6" non-stick skillet. Pour 1/4 cup of batter into the warmed pan and let it cook 2-3 minutes. Flip and cook this for another 2 minutes. Look, it's a mini crepe! Serve them warm with blueberry syrup. Do not fear the crepe. You can do this.

Fairy Blueberry Sauce... This syrupy sauce is cheerful and happy, like little fairies dancing in your mouth.

2 cups fresh blueberries
1/4 cup water
1/4 cup sugar
1/2 cup water
zest of one lemon

In a small saucepan, boil blueberries and 1/4 cup water. Simmer for about 8 minutes, until the berries are soft enough to crush with a spoon. In a separate saucepan, add sugar, water and lemon zest. Bring to a boil for one minute and cool a bit. Then mix the glaze and sauce until they're happy together. This will keep in the fridge for up to two weeks. But you will probably use it up way before then.

I just read this chapter to Ron, and as you can imagine he wasn't too terribly interested in the girly spa-ing thing, but he loves me, so he patiently let me read to him. Then he casually responded, "You know what recipe you should add to this chapter?"

What? Was he really contributing to the Ahh... the Spa chapter? He's pretty funny. He suggested spa-nakopita! Those little, puffy, flakey, triangular dynamos with a bold Mediterranean flavour. A classic Greek appetizer. Ron believes in my spanakopita. He's told me that for 33 years. I'm Greek, I cut my teeth on spanakopita. At Greek school.

Opa! Spa-nakopita!

With a side of Greek School

Now, this may look like a long recipe, but it's not. I go off on a few tangents.

> Tangent number one. Let's get a few things straight right off the top of this cooking lesson. I'm going to take you to Greek school with me for a few minutes.

You're about to learn how to make spanaKOpita. Not spanakopEEEta. Do you get it? The accent goes on the KO, not the EEE. So let's try saying that all together now girls... spanaKOpita. Good, well done. Brrrravo!

> Tangent number two. While we're at this, let's learn one more commonly mispronounced Greek word. Baklava. The magical Mediterranean dessert that calls for 87 cups of sugar and 34 cups of butter. BaklaVA. Please, not bakLAva. Please no. Or you won't be allowed to eat any. Thank you.

Now back to my Mom's recipe for authentic Greek... Opa! Spanakopita.

In the freezer section of your favourite grocery store you should find a box of phyllo dough. (Oh my, another Greek school lesson. PhEEEllo.) Buy the phyllo, a pound of unsalted butter, two cups of good quality Greek feta, one cup of cottage cheese and a bunch of fresh, I repeat FRESH spinach.

You'll also need a little bit of fresh or dried dill and two eggs. Now head home dreaming of the Mediterranean.

Don't plan on making your spanakopita right away. You'll need to defrost the phyllo in the refrigerator for at least eight hours. Don't attempt to unfold it while it's frozen. It'll break and you'll cry. Trust me I know this. Do something else during the defrosting time. If it's autumn, make leaf placemats from Chapter 2. Better yet, prepare the filling for your Opa! Spanakopita.

This is what you'll do. Wash, dry and chop the spinach. Into a large bowl it goes. Crumble the feta. In it goes too, along with the cottage cheese, the eggs and dill. I love a good shot of ground black pepper. No salt. Feta is salty. Add a dash of nutmeg, a very Greek move, but to be honest, I don't add the nutmeg. My mother always does. Blend this filling well and set it aside.

Melt about one cup of butter. Find a pastry brush and the kitchen scissors in your (messy) utensil drawer.

Get out one clean tea towel. Not a terry cloth one though. And dampen it lightly. Oh little sheet of phyllo, you're about to be wrapped in a damp, soft towel, and then gently massaged with a warm butter bath. Your phyllo is about to go to the spa before it becomes your spa-nakopita spa-night food!

I'm sorry, but you're still not quite ready to make your little spanakopita. But you're so close. Open the package of phyllo and lay the entire thing out on the counter. Using your handy kitchen scissors, cut through all 16 or so layers of phyllo creating two-inch strips width-wise. Keep one stack by your side and take the rest to the spa. What I mean is cover them with the lightly dampened towel to keep them from drying out. Just like the spa.

At long last you're now ready to make your very first spanakopita. Working quickly, but calmly, take two strips of phyllo and lightly brush each one with some butter. Don't saturate it, but don't be skimpy either. (I hope you're never dressed skimpily!) Then place one strip on top of the other. Plop one teaspoon of the fragrant filling at the bottom corner of the phyllo. Carefully fold your spanakopita into a little triangle by folding one corner over the filling. Then flip that triangle up. And then over again. See the triangle forming?

Have I confused you? At this point I really wish you could come to my kitchen and I'd show you how to fold them. We'd have tea and chat. And eat a dozen of these straight out of the oven. Tangent.

Let's try this from another angle. Do you know the proper way to fold a flag? That's how you make a spanakopita. Still not sure? I suggest you find a good flag-folding website and follow those instructions for your spanakopita folding adventures.

Before you know it, you'll soon be turning out these little darlings with speed and ease. Repeat this procedure over and over until you're done. Place them on a lightly buttered baking sheet. If you have melted butter left over, you can brush it on top of your appetizers before they head into the oven at 350° F. for about 15 minutes or until they're golden brown and puffy.

Warning: When these Grecian beauties come out of the oven, the filling is very hot. Please wait at least five short minutes before sampling.

Completely cool the ones you don't eat. They freeze very well between layers of waxed paper in a container. I do it all the time. To reheat, please follow these directions. Seriously, I've done this 1,000 times. Pre-heat the oven to 400° F. and then turn it off. Spread your defrosted spanako-pita on a baking sheet and pop them in for about 10-15 minutes. Keep an eye on them, they're already baked and you only want to reheat them. Oh please, don't reheat them in the microwave. All your hard work will turn soggy and mushy. No microwaving allowed.

Now, after that very lengthy spanakopita building lesson, there's one other speedier way you can prepare these. These will be more of a knife and fork appetizer or main course. You can simply cut your phyllo to fit into an 8" x 8" or 9" x 13" pan with a lightly buttered bottom and sides. Place about 8 sheets of phyllo in the pan buttering each one as you go along. After you have built a good foundation, spread on a thick layer of filling and repeat this layering process with another 8 sheets of phyllo. Use up any left over butter for the top and chill this for about 1/2 hour until the butter has hardened. Don't skip that step. When I discovered this miraculous move it changed my culinary life. Here's why, my Grecian goddesses.

By allowing the top layer of butter to harden in the refrigerator you can easily slice it into slick pieces before you bake it without cracking the phyllo. If you try to cut the spanakopita after it's baked, be prepared for some cracking and flying phyllo in your kitchen. This little trick works beautifully for baklava as well.

Back to your spanakopita in a pan. After it's chilled and cut, pop it into the oven at 375° F. for about 30 minutes or so. Freezing works well, but honestly, fresh and hot right out of the oven is truly the best way to serve this radiant dish. Radiant.

That was very long. I feel like we went to Greece and back together. I hope you'll give spanakopita a try at your next gathering. And please remember to pronounce it correctly. It'll all taste better if you do, I guarantee it. OPA!

Here's the background on Boaz. I've mentioned his name several times in the book and earlier in this chapter. You can find this gentleman tucked into the Old Testament. Boaz is one of the key characters in Ruth, the eighth book of the Bible.

There are many respectable adjectives I can use to describe this man of integrity- noble, upright, sensitive, caring, responsible. Please go to the book of Ruth one rainy afternoon and read about him for yourself, and see why I consider him worth mentioning.

Twenty

Baby Talk

Luke 2:19 But Mary treasured all these things, pondering them in her heart.

As a mother, I take many of the experiences with our children and store them in my heart, revisiting them from time to time. I reflect on all that's transpired by God's grace over the years. I'm so thankful that God's given us the example of Mary, a young woman who exalted the Lord, and was wise to reflect on the presence of God in her life.

Today I'm touched as I ponder another area where God has worked in our family life to draw us into a deeper relationship with Him, and also with one another.

Thank you for making room in your full day to read about His goodness to us. My prayer is that you'll seek Christ alone to be your life. Have I mentioned I love Jesus?

We love to look at baby pictures of our children who I believe were truly the most darling little things ever. Brooklynne gazes at photographs and sighs longingly as she wonders what it was like to be a baby. In fact all of our children have felt the same way, but perhaps not as passionately as Brooklynne.

Many years ago I learned that all the children loved to hear baby stories about themselves. So when they needed a laugh, some encouragement or a reminder of how much they were loved, I knew what to do. Telling baby stories was an idea that often popped into my head as a way to show our children, "You are cherished and special to us."

This may sound very basic, but how often do you really take the time to intentionally reach back into your blurry memory bank of baby days to share those fond times with your children? How will they know about their babyhood if we don't tell them? How often do you praise God for the gift of your children?

Just for today, let's not talk about the times they smeared lotions on mirrors or stomped on boxes of cereal in the kitchen or locked babysitters out of the house or faked broken limbs or conducted science experiments on the baby or stuffed peas up their nose or peeled wallpaper off the walls or decorated the bathroom with baby powder or spun the baby around until she...

Whenever our friends James and Melissa came over with their new baby, I could count on our teenage children to urge me to tell them stories about their baby days. This story telling would inevitably result in some hilarious, touching and legendary memoirs that seemed to go on for hours.

The children never tired of hearing the same adorable tales over and over. Jamison always wanted to hear one particular story about when he was my kitchen helper. As a toddler, he was always excited to stand on the kitchen stool by my side as I prepared a meal. But he'd begin to fidget and often the stool would slip out an inch or so. He'd grip the counter for dear life and franticly exclaim, "Jamo fall down, Jamo fall down!" Seriously girlfriends, I can still hear the terror in his little voice. Here's another winner. When he was very little he referred to his snow-suit as his snow-snoot! How cute is that? As a 20-something-year-old, he still relishes these sweet stories of his baby days. I do too.

I absolutely need to tell you one more precious story about Jamison, who obviously knew right from wrong at a very early age. He could only have been about a year-and-a-half old when he had a new little buddy over for playtime. His friend was just a year old.

For some unknown reason I went upstairs for a second (not such a good idea) and after minute or so I could hear Jamison repeatedly sighing loudly, and making heavy huffing and puffing sounds. As I headed down to where they were, I saw a very distraught Jamison, standing in a pile of dirt, trying to physically pull the visitor away from a large floor plant in the kitchen. His little friend had found some pleasure in digging up the soil in my plant. Jamison knew that was not acceptable behaviour. In his frustration he looked up at me with his intense brown eyes and in a troubled tone of voice, simply exclaimed over and over, "baby uh-oh, baby uh-oh!" At one-and-a-half he had a limited vocabulary, but baby uh-oh was something he could articulate well. This is known as the "baby uh-oh" story in our home. Maybe you had to be there. But I choose to believe Jamison had great wisdom from God as a toddler.

Brooklynne loved to hear that as a two year old she would ask for chicken noonal oop (Translation: chicken noodle soup.) Genevieve always laughed about the time she shoved peas up into her nose and had to be taken to emergency at the hospital. And Alexandra relished stories about her trea-sured Teddy who "melled" (Translation: smelled.) She would sniff him and then tell me, "Teddy mells." He did. It was gross. I washed him often.

You know, dear friend, I could go on for pages telling you about all the adorable things my chil-dren said and did. But that would be very obnox-ious of me. We've been through the obnoxious issues together in Chapter 9!

Hmm... instead, may I suggest you reflect on the special moments from your child's baby days that you've hidden in your heart? I know you have them treasured up somewhere in your head, behind the memories of sleepless nights and colossal laundry piles. Ponder those baby stories, then share them with your child and see his or her face brighten up.

I wonder if Mary told Jesus about the holy night He was born, about the glorious angel choir conducted by the very hand of God and the first guests who rushed to welcome the King of kings to earth? I've been thinking about something. We women love to share stories with each other. If we gathered around a fire with Mary, can you imagine the tender baby stories she'd share with us, in a soft and loving voice, about raising the Son of God?

This chapter is called Baby Talk. My friend, go for it, take the time to talk baby talk with your grown up baby. And in it all, praise God, the Creator of life who gave you all these times with your children. It'll be time well spent. That's something to ponder.

Twenty-One

Coffee and Cookies
with the Boys

**Psalm 119:9 How can a young man keep his
way pure? By keeping it according
to Your word.**

John was a former Irish terrorist.
He spoke with an incredible passion for Jesus
at our church one Sunday morning. In his testimony he told us how God took him from a life of
terror, to a life of trust in Jesus Christ. He shared
how he'd laid down his weapons and picked up
the Sword. Then he talked about how God showed
him that after all the senseless death and blood
he'd seen in his life as a former terrorist, he could
look to the one death that had a purpose- One
whose blood was shed for everlasting life.

It wasn't long into his testimony that Sunday
when the Lord gave me a *(gasp) I have an idea!*
moment. We had to have this man into our home
to speak to a gathering of young men. I can't tell

you how much I love it when the Lord impresses these ideas on my heart. I enjoy Jesus. Do you enjoy Jesus?

A few weeks later we ran a small announcement in the church bulletin that said, "Former Irish terrorist pays visit to Gladysz home next Sunday night. All youth boys welcome." Sometimes the very predictable church bulletin needs to be livened up.

On that warm Sunday evening I smiled as I taped a sign to our front door that said, "Former Terrorist Meeting here at 7:00 p.m. Please come in."

Ron, a great host, warmly greeted the young men at the door as I made coffee and plated cookies in the kitchen. After all, we were hoping to create a casual atmosphere so our guests would linger after the meeting. Jamison, who's also a natural host, introduced his hockey, lacrosse, youth group, music, school and neighbourhood friends to each other.

Our spacious living room quickly filled up with teenage boys. Some sat quietly on our white sofas and others arranged themselves on my grandmother's antique oriental carpet. The overflow sat in rows in the dining room. There was an awkward silence and the body language screamed uncertainty. Only a few dared to even whisper.

Seated on the very edge of one sofa was our new friend John, who looked quite eager to see a room full of young men. His sweet wife, a dignified woman with a delicate smile, sat lovingly beside him, seemingly unaware of the male presence surrounding her. I could see them carefully scan the room. Finally Ron gave the nod to begin the evening, one that we'd sensed the Lord had been planning for a few weeks. And with that, all eyes and ears turned to the mysterious little man on the sofa.

The boys in our living room sat riveted and motionless, in utter silence as our friend told shocking tales of violence, atrocities and bloodshed. He bounced around on the sofa as he shared his stories. His stately wife sat calmly by his side in support. He talked about hatred, brutality and how resentment over his small stature led him into violent actions.

After several hours John sat back, looking convinced that the teenagers had heard that with one simple choice, they could have a life unlike anything they could ever imagine. He told them about the benefits of letting someone else take over their lives. It was the same remarkable testimony of Christ he'd given at church. He confidently answered questions from the few who dared to ask, as the rest headed straight to the kitchen for cookies. Our guests left and I took the sign off the front door, pleased with how well the night had gone and exhilarated by the great turnout for this unusual get together.

Over the years I've often thought about that unconventional evening, wondering how Christ used it in the lives of those young men, but only God knows such things and we rest in that. Our responsibility was to hear God's instruction and obey His command.

Would you dare to ask God whom He'd choose to bring into your home if you opened it up one night for His kingdom? Would you dare ask your church to run an atypical announcement in your Sunday bulletin for the sake of His work? What sign would you dare tape to your front door for an evening that would bring Him glory?

I have a loaf recipe that I've been making, baking and taking for 33 years. It is exquisite. I love it so much that recently I spent the day and night fiddling around with the loaf and turned it into a cookie recipe especially for you. The cookies are a merry-go-round of flavours and textures. With reverence, I've named these cookies...

O Taste and see that the LORD is Good Cookies

2 cups whole wheat flour
2 t. baking powder
1/4 cup wheat germ
1/2 t. salt
1/3 cup softened butter
1 cup brown sugar
2 eggs
1 t. vanilla
2 T. lemon zest (do not skip this one)
1/2 cup orange juice
1 cup mashed bananas (about 3 really ripe ones)
3/4 cup chopped nuts

3/4 cup mixed dried fruit, our favourites are cherries, apricots, pears and peaches (venture away from the usual raisins and cranberries)

Just telling you about these makes me praise Jesus.

Combine the dry ingredients: flour, baking powder, wheat germ, and salt. Cream together the butter, sugar, eggs, vanilla, lemon, orange juice and bananas. Add the nuts and dried fruit. Then blend both mixtures together well, but don't overdo it.

Drop a heaping tablespoonful of the cookie batter onto a greased or parchment-lined cookie sheet. I really, really like parchment paper. It makes me feel like a professional baker. I find myself pretending to be on the Food Channel. Pop the cookies into your 350° F. oven for about 12 minutes. They'll be a bit soft and lusciously golden. Here's something I've discovered. The flavours in these cookies get better and better the longer they play around together. Hide them for a few days and then have a great cookie unveiling for your family.

Twenty-Two

Avocado Green makes a Comeback

John 15:4 Abide in Me, and I in you. As the branch cannot bear fruit of itself unless it abides in the vine, so neither can you unless you abide in Me.

I always looked forward to my Tuesday night tidy-up because it was the one time of the week when housecleaning became a joy and a privilege.

After the children were all tucked in, I couldn't wait to polish the washroom and scatter a bit of dust off the coffee tables. I vacuumed the family room with more zest than ever on my Tuesday night tidy-ups. Then I'd turn my attention to setting up my avocado green, 36 cup coffee pot, an heirloom from my mother's 1970's kitchen. I could arrange coffee mugs and a variety of teas with such gusto on Tuesday nights.

Even after a long day of mothering, chauffeuring, catering, laundering, negotiating and tutoring, God gave me more than enough energy to transform the command central area of our home into what my friends called, a haven of refreshment, for our Wednesday morning ladies Bible study.

The last thing I did before heading to bed would be to set up chairs in a large circle around the family room. As I turned off the lights and headed up to bed, the Lord would put a holy readiness and peaceful eagerness in my heart for the coming morning. I couldn't wait until daybreak.

As each Wednesday morning greeted me, I'd have the honour of welcoming over a dozen women into our home. We'd gather before God to deepen our relationship with Him through the study of His profound Word, and to love one another through prayer. We'd come to Him looking for wisdom and truth, confessing our need for His indwelling in our lives. Girls, it was a beautiful time. You know what I'm talking about if you've ever been in a Bible study with other women. If you haven't, you should find one. Today.

All the women used the gifts God had given them for His purposes on those special mornings. One dear sister in Christ served the Lord by babysitting all the toddlers and preschoolers in our playroom for several hours while we studied and prayed. One wise sister would lead the study, another would organize our missions prayer time and others took turns providing delicious breakfast snacks. Mmm... we always had good food. For about five years, from September until June, this was our sacred time to abide together in Christ.

The ladies in this Bible study had a long history together before I met them. Decades.

However, shortly after I joined in, the time came for the group to find a new home in which to meet weekly. That's when God moved and there I was at a *(gasp) I have* an *idea!* point with the Lord again. My hand went up and within seconds I was the new hostess of the Bible study for the coming fall. I love fall, Bible study and Jesus. What a combination.

All summer long I kept going over and over with the Lord what a great idea He'd given me the morning He volunteered me to open our home for His purposes. I couldn't wait to turn the calendar page to that first September morning when I knew our home would be filled with women, Bibles and babies, coffee and conversation, accented with the pleasing aroma of voices lifted up to God in prayer. I could sense the air of prayer that would soon permeate our home.

Sorry if that all sounds a bit dramatic. But today, 15 years later, I still recall the passion God cultivated in my heart for offering hospitality to these sisters in Christ. What better way could there be to build a house, than by wisdom and knowledge, so that the rooms could be filled with all precious and pleasant riches? (You have to read Proverbs 24:3 & 4! Go ahead take a few minutes to open your Bible and mediate on that gem.)

One fall, winter and spring, led to another fall, winter and spring, which led to another fall, winter and spring of Bible studies in our family room. Being the hostess was effortless, only because God had me totally focused on serving Him in our home. I rejoiced as I greeted my sisters of the Southeast Bible Study and Prayer Cell week after week, month after month, year after year.

Oh, the vintage, avocado green coffee pot and the vacuum cleaner got a workout each week. And every Wednesday morning we took big steps towards living lives in the fullness of Christ, while the preschoolers took little steps together in our playroom in a united effort to release every toy and book from its place. God bless our sister, Joan, who selflessly and patiently cared for those little ones over the years.

Here's where the story gets even better.

Our Brooklynne was a sweet little preschooler during the years we held the Bible study in our home. Even as a wee one, she knew the Wednesday morning routine. As she came down the stairs on those days she'd see the usual circle of chairs, along with the avocado green artifact and coffee for the masses. Women and children were on the way. Weekly I prayed God would be glorified through this study and prayer time. But I had no idea of how He'd also use this offering to influence her young life. Hold that thought.

Time passed.

One day during Brooklynne's last year in high school, she burst through the door into the family room happily chattering about her day. Suddenly she stopped and fell silent. As she looked around the family room and into the kitchen she spoke four profound words with boldness and confidence that still resound in my head today.

"Well, there's my childhood," she proclaimed, and then she proceeded to weave her way around the maze of chairs and up to her room.

I'll explain. I was having a group of ladies over for a meeting that night. I'd set up the family room in that familiar circle of chairs and there was a coffee party waiting to happen on the kitchen table. Brooklynne's response to this sight triggered her memory to rewind to those days of cookies and milk, women and the Word. Her words, "Well, there's my childhood," penetrated my heart as a mother so deeply and with such intensity that I simply can't put my emotions into words. Trust me I've tried.

I'm in awe of Christ, that He'd cause Brooklynne to equate a simple circle of chairs in our home, with her childhood and serving the Lord. Numerous times since then I've gone over those words, which God spoke to me through her that afternoon. They were for her benefit and mine. She acknowledged once again that Christ has been at work in her life since her childhood. God showed me how far reaching His love is for us, especially when we choose to hear and obey Him in our lives.

The avocado trophy has long since been replaced with a shiny stainless steel 2011 model coffee pot. The little ones who destroyed our play-room are college graduates and we mothers have Bibles with well-worn pages. But the truths God taught us during our Southeast Bible Study and Prayer Cell times will remain rooted in our hearts all the days of our lives. Look how God causes all things to work together for good to those who love him.

Need a good idea of how to use your home for God's glory? Host a Bible study in your home and wait to see what God will do.

One morning my beloved friend Bev, brought these sweetie-pies to Bible study and life has never been the same. Do not delay, make these today. I tend to rename recipes. I lovingly named these...

Bev's Breakfast Beauties

8 oz. cream cheese, softened
1 egg yolk
1 t. vanilla
1 1/4 cup white or brown sugar, divided
1 T. lemon zest (this is an option, a good option)
1 loaf white or whole wheat sandwich bread, with crusts removed please
1 T. cinnamon
1/2 cup melted butter (butter!)

Combine the cream cheese, egg, vanilla, 1/4 cup sugar and lemon zest in a bowl. Blend this up well. Flatten each slice of bread with a rolling pin and spread 1 tablespoon of the cream cheese filling on each one. Roll diagonally from point to point. Get the point?

Mix the remaining sugar and cinnamon together on a plate and dip each little roll in the butter and then the cinnamon-sugar goodness. Pop them onto an ungreased cookie sheet and bake these beauties at 350° F. for 15-17 minutes. You can serve them warm or at room temperature. Warm is best. They freeze really well, I do it all the time. I may go make some right now.

Twenty-Three

Listen UP

Philippians 4:8 Finally, brethren, whatever is true, whatever is honorable, whatever is right, whatever is pure, whatever is lovely, whatever is of good repute, if there is any excellence and if anything worthy of praise, dwell on these things.

The sound of an Adventures in Odyssey CD billowing out of your child's room at bedtime.

The sound of majestic Christmas music playing softly in the living room.

The sound of contemporary Christian music helping with homework in a teenager's bedroom.

The sound of a preacher's voice on a laptop retelling Sunday's message.

The sound of a worship CD humming in the background of your kitchen.

The sound of Christian satellite radio permeating your home.

These are some of the sounds of Christ in our homes.

I'll admit I was somewhat unsure of myself as I sat down to write this short segment today. But as soon as I confessed my unsure-of-myselfness, God showed me He's my strength. Remember those great words from the classic childhood hymn? "I am weak, but He is strong" As I write, God reminds me that even at 50-something, I am weak but He is strong. A thought well worth pondering for a while.

This idea suddenly came to me back in the days when our home was brimming with children, which also meant it was filled with a melting pot of melt-downs, the horror of hormones, plus emotions and lotions.

The idea: When I have the sounds of Christ playing in our home, I've personally found that it's more likely that I'll demonstrate the fruit of the Spirit... love, joy, peace, patience, kindness, goodness, faithfulness, gentleness and self-control with our children, my husband or whoever's bugging me. I'm serious. It's harder to go crazy on the people around me with the sweet sounds of Jesus in the air.

Now wouldn't you agree with me, that's a good idea? It's God's idea not mine, so that's why I can confidently say it's a good one. How can a mother yell at her children with the compassionate voice of John Avery Whittaker in the background? Or the hallowed voices of a Christmas choir? Or Rebecca St.James singing Breathe? I'm not a yeller, (oh sister, I have other issues for sure) but I'll just say there was maybe once or twice when I wished I'd had some of the sounds of Jesus on in the background.

Writing about the sounds in and around our home reminds me of some dynamic melodies that ascended from our basement during Jamison's high school years. Are some of you already nodding as you envision where I'm going with this?

Our creative son is a musician. He began playing the violin when he was four years old and received his first drum set when he was six. As he grew, so did his resumé of musical interests... piano, guitar and voice training. In high school his repertoire of music genres included vocal jazz, chamber choir, jazz bands and symphonic winds groups. Our basement housed rehearsals for worship bands and noisy musical groups. When your son's the drummer, you automatically sign yourself up for the rehearsal venue!

There are some major cracks in the walls of our basement from those high school years. And not because of wild parties. Let's just say during band practice I had to take the phone with me and sit on the front stairs if I wanted to make a call. The band was called Restrain The Enemy and it was made up of the finest group of young teenage boys a mother could ever ask for. Noise and all, I really liked band practice days. I'm weird.

The boys in the band were always polite and as soon as they arrived they'd thank me for allowing them to have band practice in our home. Little did they know that one day they'd be written up in a pink women's inspirational book! I loved having all those sweaty boys laughing and eating chips in our basement. But here was my favourite part. When I heard a break in the music, I'd cautiously open the door and invite myself down into their world of amps, cords, microphones and unique boy odours. Every time I descended the stairs, in unison, they'd cheer "juice time!" They knew my appearance meant cold juice and cookies. Did I mention they were a bit sweaty?

The Lord blessed my heart with each cookie and glass of juice I served. Girls, they were teenage boys who loved Jesus, sang about Him and got excited over juice! You read that right, juice! I'm not suggesting if you're looking for a way to use your home for the kingdom, that you need to find a band, make some snacks and serve cold drinks. But I am going to say that we all need to live a life yielded to Christ. Plain and simple. That might mean sweaty boys and noisy music. But I do believe I've read somewhere we are to make a joyful noise unto the Lord.

Hmm... getting back to my first point. When the "sounds" of Jesus are playing in our home, I experience God's presence at my side and I'm not as likely to lose it. If you know what I mean. I'll close with some words for you to ponder, breathed by the greatest Author I know.

Psalm 150:6 Let everything that has breath praise the LORD. Praise the LORD!

Twenty-Four

No Thank you

Ecclesiastes 3:1 There is an appointed time for everything. And there is a time for every event under heaven...

I'm not joking when I say that I think our children went from skinned knees to car keys almost overnight.

Somehow all four of our children grew up too quickly. I've spoken with many mothers who agree that the high school years appeared to go even faster than any of the previous ones. For some parents that was a blessing, but the rest of us wondered who put life in fast-forward. Septembers came at me faster and faster each year. Who was turning the pages on my calendar when I wasn't looking?

What I'm about to say may come as no surprise to you, but I will openly admit that when our oldest daughter, Genevieve began her grade 12 year, I cried. Often. As I stood in the puddle from my gushing heart, I realized things were happening too quickly. Come on now girlfriend, you have to agree with me that children grow up far too fast. I know there's nothing profound in that familiar statement, but I just had to write it.

In the spring of Genevieve's 12th grade, I didn't like getting the mail because suddenly applications became acceptances. I needed more time with her.

Time. That's how God gently captivated my heart for a new and tender idea. One that was far more profitable than tears. He showed me that I needed to intentionally free up some of my time in order to be available to Genevieve, and to look back on her last year at home with no regrets.

Ladies, oh, how the Lord works when we're yielded to Him. He enabled me to see where and how to realistically free up some time in my life. By His grace, I was able to stand firm in my decision to not take on any more responsibilities, especially leadership roles, and to apply more wisdom as I made decisions regarding my time.

I wrote a few letters, made a few calls and the Lord made more room in my life than I could've ever imagined. We had three younger children who were all still enjoying their extra-curricular activities, so I certainly wasn't sitting around in the evenings gazing glassy-eyed at Genevieve as she did her homework. I was still immersed in all our children's lives, and committed to their commitments.

I graciously declined any larger responsibilities and volunteer positions that year. And look at how God worked! As I shared a little bit about my "no thank you, I decline" stage with my friends, I wasn't surprised to hear that so many women longed to free up time to devote to their homes and children, especially as they watched graduation day rapidly approaching.

Two years later we found ourselves marking another graduation date on the calendar. That September my sweet friends watched to see if I'd use the same blueprint with our second daughter, Alexandra, and once again God led me back to His original idea. I stepped back, stepped down and said "no thanks."

I cherished my extra time at home in the evenings with the children for much needed conversations, not just talks. I perfected my smoothie making skills and served many platters. (Remember Chapter 16?) I was more available to all the children for applications, calculations, admirations, conversations, demonstrations, expectations, explanations, fascinations, hesitations, observations, preparations, registrations, revelations, situations and speculations.

All I had done to make more free time was to simply say, "no thank you, not this year." I have no regrets for taking a year off each time we had a graduate, especially because I began to see how each child looked forward to hearing I'd be doing less volunteering and disappearing.

And so dear little friend, I have nothing fancy to write or flashy to say other than to ask you one question. During an appointed time, would you step away from whatever the volunteer sign up sheet is in your life, if that was the direction the Lord was leading you?

Twenty-Five

31,103

2 Timothy 3:16 All Scripture is inspired by God and profitable for teaching, for reproof, for correction, for training in righteousness...

31,103. Any guesses?

- The number of germs on my kitchen counter? No. That's gross.
- The number of e-mails I've sent to our children since the first one left home? No. I've probably sent more.
- The number of centimeters of snow we got this winter in Saskatchewan? No. I think we measure snow by the ton in this province.
- The number of mosquitoes in our backyard in the month of July? No, I'm sure there are more than that.
- The number of golf balls I lose in a season? No. But that's pretty close.

Ron did a little research for me one morning when I was trying to come up with a snazzy name for the small group of teenage girls I worked with at our church. I finally chose the name SG31,103 for our group. The girls were stumped trying to guess the significance of this name. I gave them one hint- SG did not stand for Stephanie Gladysz! It stood for "small group."

31,103 are the total number of verses in the Bible. God's given us His Word to teach, reproof, correct and train us in righteousness. You can read that for yourselves in 2 Timothy 3:16 & 17. While you're at it, why not read the whole chapter? Or all of 2 Timothy?

What a gift! Right there in your hand you hold 31,103 verses written by the Lord God Almighty so that you may be adequate and equipped for every good work.

One blessed day, oh so many years ago, God kindly gave me a *(gasp) I have an idea!* instant that caused my heart to leap for joy. Since God knows I love to work a theme around anything, He showed me how to use His Word as a theme.

Romans 15:13 says, "Now may the God of hope fill you with all joy and peace in believing, so that you will abound in hope by the power of the Holy Spirit." This became the verse I prayed for Genevieve as she graduated and went to Bible school. I've prayed those powerful words for her many times since then and it's become the verse I still go back to 10 years later as I intercede for her.

When Alexandra left home for college, we sent her with our blessing and Psalm 92:12 & 13. "The righteous man will flourish like the palm tree, he will grow like a cedar in Lebanon. Planted in the house of the LORD, they will flourish in the courts of our God."

For our only son, the Lord reminded me of Psalm 119:9. "How can a young man keep his way pure? By keeping it according to Your word." As he's grown into a young man, I've prayed this for him year after year. Everyday. This morning while I was on the treadmill.

After Brooklynne graduated I began praying Psalm 84:11 for her. "For the LORD God is a sun and shield; the LORD gives grace and glory; no good thing does He withhold from those who walk uprightly."

All the children know I've been led to pray a particular verse for them. Whether their day has been a mess or a success, they can rest in the Lord knowing there's a daily prayer lifted up to the throne room of heaven for them.

There are 31,103 verses God has spoken to us and for us. If you inquire of the Lord, He'll lead you through His Word and will speak to you. He really will. Whether you are studying a word, phrase, sentence, verse, passage, chapter or book, seek God with all your heart. If it's His will, He may even lead you to that one special verse for that one special child on that one special occasion; don't be surprised if you too have a (gasp) that's the verse! moment.

When you've discovered the good news of God's Word, don't keep it to yourself. Let your children know which verses you're praying for them and why. I've found that as I study and pray Scripture for the children, the eyes of my heart are enlightened and He shows me His surpassing greatness towards me. That is a gift.

Twenty-Six

Do the Hokey Pokey

Colossians 1:29 For this purpose also I labor, striving according to His power, which mightily works within me.

I can't land a double axel, but I can join in quite comfortably on a sunny winter afternoon for a family skate date. I'm not a marathon runner, but I can run a couple of miles, slowly. You won't find me on the expert runs (unless I take a wrong turn) on the ski hill, but I can keep up with the children on the intermediate slopes. I'm not busting out in front of the pack on an afternoon bike ride, but I'm somewhere in the middle. I'm sure not at the gym seven days a week, but my gym bag and I do go on outings together several mornings a week. I'm not on the LPGA tour, but I can occasionally make par. Maybe once or twice. (May I please add something here? I took up golf when I turned 50 and during the fifth round of golf I'd ever played in my life, I made a hole in one on a par 3! It's true, there were three witnesses. I even made the sports section of the newspaper. Thanks for letting me share that.)

I'm constantly aware that it's only because of Christ in me that I can do any of these things. It's surely not me, but His strength in me. His energy.

Now girls, take a minute and look at all those activities I listed off at the start. Each one of them can be done with your children, or grandchildren if you're really fit. One of my ambitions in life is to stay in shape to be able to be active with our children and eventually, grandchildren.

Ron and I have both skied since we were teenagers. He's improved and you'll find him on the black diamond runs. I still look for the blue dot runs, where I'm perfectly content and happy to still be in one piece at the end of a day on the slopes.

Thirty years ago, before children, when we'd ski Banff every weekend, something interesting caught my eye on the mountain. Naturally, I stood in awe of the majesty of the Lord on the mountaintop. But what else really impressed me were the parents and grandparents skiing with their children. I recall a *(gasp) I have an idea!* moment and thinking, I want that, someday when it's our turn. As a young bride, my heart's cry was to be physically active with our children when we had our family.

God gave us four healthy children and the desire of my heart to be "actively" involved in their lives only grew stronger as they grew older. But, sister, this body did some growing as well. You know what I'm talking about! So as a young mom I decided that if one day I wanted to be that grandparent on the ski hill with my grandchild, I had to get fit and stay fit way before that time.

Unfortunately, ladies, that doesn't just happen. It takes a bit of hard work, a little extra time and some discipline. That's all! It doesn't have to be expensive or elaborate. The goal is to get moving! Do the hokey pokey. Some of you will have to google that.

You've heard it said many times before. Walk, run or jump up and down with joy. Get active three times a week. We hear this in the media. I'm not going to give you a fitness plan or exercise regime. I know you can figure that out. I'm here to give you a loving push. Who doesn't want to be limber enough to play with a baby and some toys on the floor? Or skate along side your child at a family skate. You get the picture?

Let me tell you a story. It's a bit of a hard one for me to write, but I will. This winter I shoveled the snow six times. I had an absolute blast. Last month Ron and I took our children skiing for the day. It was a magnificent day for me on the slopes. This week I've been to the gym twice and can't wait to go back tomorrow. So what? Big deal? Yes, in fact it's a very big deal.

A year and a half ago I was suddenly diagnosed with colon cancer. I had surgery and then six months of chemotherapy, which ended about nine months ago. So shoveling and skiing are a very big deal. I'll never again complain about shoveling. There was a season in my life that I couldn't do a whole lot of anything, but God healed me, praise Him, praise Him, PRAISE HIM! Being active again has a new meaning in my life. I share this with you to give God the utmost glory and to use my story to encourage you to "move" while you are able. Do lots of things while you are able. There's so much more to this story, but that's all for now. Perhaps there's another book to be written.

Now, back to your running shoes.

Proverbs 31:17 says, "She girds herself with strength and makes her arms strong." Hmm... nowhere in Proverbs 31 is there any mention of the worthy woman's appearance. The only hint we have about her physique is that her arms are strong. And so we can ask the Lord to make our arms strong for the tasks He sets before us. Ladies, we need to do our part too, so let's look after ourselves.

Take another look at Colossians 1:29. "For this purpose also I labor, striving according to His power, which mightily works within me." The New International Version describes it as being according to His "energy." It's not our own strength, energy or power, it's all His. And He doesn't run out. So when you think you're running out of energy, remember it's not yours anyhow. Any energy we have is His, whatever the task.

As I ponder and reflect on the many blessings we've enjoyed together as an active family, I thank God for His smile upon us. He has truly given me the desires of my heart's cry from that mountaintop three decades ago. Today, as a married woman of some 30ish years, my prayer is still the same as it was as a young bride- I still want to be active with our children and someday, our children's children.

Friends, I smile as I think of you moving too... moving yourself closer to the Lord and deeper into His Word. Oh just wait and see what ideas He has for you and your family! **Warning:** you may gasp.

Twenty-Seven

Boaz or Bozo?

**Proverbs 6:20 & 21 My son, observe the
commandment of your father
And do not forsake the teaching
of your mother;
Bind them continually on your heart;
Tie them around your neck.**

It was a lazy hazy summer day when God bestowed upon me a *(gasp) I have an idea!* moment. Jamison was not yet a teenager, but 'twas a very precious season for me as I observed our boy beginning to man-up right before my very eyes.

The Lord got me thinking about how we were raising our son. As a Boaz or a Bozo? Does anyone want to raise a Bozo? I think not. (Remember Boaz? We talked about him in Chapter 19 and you read about him in the book of Ruth.)

Because of Christ's life in Ron, he's nurtured our son since the moment he was born. Literally. In the delivery room, when Jamison was only minutes old, Ron held him in close to his face, and talked about fishing, playing hockey and hanging out together. I'm not suggesting that fishing automatically makes a man into a chivalrous Boaz. But Ron wanted to have those special father-son times with Jamison from a young age in order to point him to Jesus and help build his little boy into a noble young man of God.

Scripture indicates that mothers also play a role in raising sons. So that summer I had the practical idea to teach Jamison the art of opening doors for women of all ages. As a mother of three daughters, I'd heard more than my share of stories about young men who missed the memo that most girls appreciate good door etiquette. Chivalry anyone?

Even though it was a sizzler of a summer, I assured Jamison my idea was not a result of heat stroke. By September he realized mothers really do know what they're talking about. Most of the time. This is how I looked at it. If there was a door, there was a teachable moment. As I fondly recall "the summer of the door," I must commend Jamison for being such a good sport. One Sunday morning in the early fall it all paid off.

As Jamison and I approached the doors of the church we met up with one of the grand older women of our congregation. Jamison politely stepped in beside us, reached over and opened the door for us. The woman passed through first and we followed her. She stopped just inside, turned around and in an astonished but joyous voice began to preach a sermonette to everyone around us. I recall her praising the Lord for polite, courteous, young men and announcing that she couldn't remember the last time a boy opened a door for her. Jamison's eyes met mine. We didn't exchange a word. He could see the smile of gratitude and motherly pride in my eyes.

I didn't have to say, "I told you so," because the Lord had provided a dear saint to emphasize the point of good door etiquette practice. Her sincere response spoke louder and sunk deeper than this mother's teaching and preaching, and preaching and teaching.

But ladies, would you agree with me that the standard we want for our boys hinges on more than just a door? As parents, we want to see our sons grow in wisdom and stature, and in favour with God and men. (Take a few minutes to read Luke 2:41-52.) I believe the lessons Jamison learned about opening doors were an open door to explore how God commands us to live.

I had some fun today as I looked up the dictionary meaning of chivalry. This is a bit of what I found. Chivalry: the sum of the ideal quality of a knight, including courtesy, generosity, valor and dexterity in arms; courage, fairness, politeness; respectful attention especially towards women. If I could add a personal note to that definition it would be... and the fear of the Lord.

Girlfriends, I believe so many of us want to see our sons display these characteristics. But chivalry is also in the minds of many young women I know. Glory to God, I've repeatedly heard our daughters and oodles of their friends declare that what they desire in a man is a Boaz rather than a Bozo.

I'm not going to give you Stephanie's Top 10 Steps to Chivalry, because those don't exist. Nor am I going to tell you how Boaz-building looked in our home. Instead, just as we pointed Jamison to Christ, I want to point you to Jesus, through God's Word.

- Proverbs 1:7... The fear of the LORD is the beginning of knowledge; fools despise wisdom and instruction.
- Proverbs 3:3... Do not let kindness and truth leave you; bind them around your neck, write them on the tablet of your heart.
- Proverbs 4:5... Acquire wisdom! Acquire understanding! Do not forget nor turn away from the words of my mouth.
- Proverbs 4:23... Watch over your heart with all diligence, for from it flow the springs of life.
- Proverbs 11:2... When pride comes, then comes dishonor, but with the humble is wisdom.
- Proverbs 22:6... Train up a child in the way he should go, even when he is old he will not depart from it.
- Galatians 6:10... So then, while we have opportunity, let us do good to all people, and especially to those who are of the household of the faith.
- Ephesians 4:29... Let no unwholesome word proceed from your mouth, but only such a word as is good for edification according to the need of the moment, so that it will give grace to those who hear.

- Ephesians 5:1 & 2... Therefore be imitators of God, as beloved children; and walk in love, just as Christ also loved you and gave Himself up for us, an offering and a sacrifice to God as a fragrant aroma.

One Christmas 20-year-old Jamison asked for a waffle maker. Ron and I were selfishly excited as we shopped for just the right one for him. You know what we were thinking. As we browsed through the kitchen appliances, we dreamt of fluffy waffles, topped with whipped cream and fresh fruit, served to us on Christmas morning by our sweet son. We were two jolly shoppers the day we headed home with our, I mean his, new waffle maker.

Since then we've been spoiled with early morning waffle-fests, lunch-brunch waffle extravaganzas and midnight waffle parties. I suggest that if your child asks for a waffle maker for Christmas, you give him a hug, tell him he's brilliant and get shopping faster than you can say... a bowl full of jelly.

Jamison's Far from Awful Waffles... (as told to me by Jamison)

5 cups waffle mix
5 cups of milk
5 eggs
5 T. of olive oil

Whisk the waffle mix and the milk together. Separate the egg whites from the yokes. Mix the yokes into the milk. The egg whites should be in a separate bowl for special treatment. NO YOKES ALLOWED. Whip those whites into soft peaks. Make them fluffy now. This is a good time to warm your waffle iron. Carefully fold the whites into the mix. Make sure not to stir. We like air in the mix to make fluffy waffles. Fluffy waffles are happy waffles. You can now add the olive oil. This makes for the crispy outside when the waffle is cooked.

Once your waffle maker is at cooking temperature, you can add the batter accordingly. I have a Belgian waffle maker that calls for a 1/3 cup of batter per quarter of the iron. Your waffle iron will most likely be different, so experiment to find which amount makes the optimal waffle. Follow cooking directions for your waffle iron in order to identify the perfectly cooked waffle. I prefer mine on the crispier side. Try different cooking times to find your preferred crispiness.

This recipe makes about 8 waffles.

It is imperative to top your waffles with good things such as whipped cream, all sorts of fruits, a variety of syrups, nuts and chocolate for the perfect waffle experience. You can also easily add fruit, nuts or even chocolate chips into the mix before filling the iron, to capitalize on your favourite texture and flavour.

Two of the most important things I've learned when making waffles, is to keep an open mind; if you think it would go well in or with a waffle, try it. Also, they're good any time of the day, no need to limit yourself to breakfast!

My turn again. Jamison uses Coyote Original or Flax Seed Waffle Mix. Turns out great every time.

Twenty-Eight

Family and Friends Feast

Hebrews 13:1 & 2 Let love of the brethren continue. Do not neglect to show hospitality to strangers, for by this some have entertained angels without knowing it.

Amen to that! I'm all about hospitality; entertaining and loving the angels I call family and friends that God has lavishly poured into our lives. I find pure joy in a good night with friends and a gooey chocolate dessert by a crackling fire, or a leisurely family breakfast with lots of coffee on our back deck under the big umbrella.

I've said it time and time again. I love our family and I love our friends. It may sound so simple, but the love I have, most certainly for our family, but also for our friends, is a passion that God ignited in my heart from our young married days and has kindled through different stages over many years.

Having proclaimed that, I'll also say that I'm always in the mood for a new idea from the Lord, especially one that will bring our family together with friends for some special times. And that's exactly what happened one summer night at our restaurant when all the children were home for a holiday. It started out small, as most ideas do, and grew into what I now call a legendary tradition, all because of the Lord's love and provision. Legendary.

Genevieve and Alexandra asked if they could have a few friends over for dinner at the restaurant. We said sure. It didn't take long for Jamison and Brooklynne to ask if they could go with the girls. Ron and I looked at each other and decided that we, too, must have a few friends who would enjoy a dinner party at the restaurant. By the time we were all seated, menus in hand, there were about 12 of us at one long table.

As I took a minute to peer over my menu and gaze down that very lively long table, God blessed me as I listened to joyous laughter and spirited conversations between family and good friends. We ate for what seemed like hours and lingered long into dessert and pots of coffee. Finally we said our goodnights and then it happened. I had an idea! This was family, these were friends, and this was a feast the Lord had laid before us. I began planning the next Family and Friends Feast in my head!

The idea took off and God has orchestrated so many Family and Friends Feasts since that first night- Christmas, Thanksgiving, Easter, summer or whenever one or more of the children come home. Their friends have been known to call us before our children arrive home to inquire what night Family and Friends Feast will be held so they can set that date aside. (I believe there are a couple of girls who've joined us in almost every Family and Friends Feast...Lyn and Elizabeth are regulars.) I love it. I love all the ideas God has given me, but this is one of my favourites. I have a lot of favourites.

Now, I think I know what you're thinking-"Stephanie, that's fine for you because you own a restaurant and you can have as many people over for dinner as often as you want and you don't have to plan and shop and clean and prepare and cook and clean up." Yes, that's all true. However, I ask you girlfriend, do you have a kitchen, living room, backyard, deck or patio? Does the city you live in have a park and trees, or is there a beach nearby? Do you have even one family member or friend? If you can answer yes to any one of these questions, then God has provided the opportunity for you to have your own Family and Friends Feast.

We've tried each of these ideas and have ended up with some wonderful times and exceptional memories. Besides your friends, all you need for your own feast is a neighbourhood park, barbeque pit, picnic table and a selection of good food. Or plan a Sunday afternoon gathering at the beach with a football, some blankets, cold watermelon, lemonade, and a few simple summer time treats.

Backyards are a perfect place to hold a get together. No need to dust or vacuum. No worrying about spills and crumbs. Everyone contributes, everyone enjoys. Voilà, you have yourself a Family and Friends Feast.

Oh and then there's the mobile feast.

One winter our family got together with another family of six and found ourselves on a spontaneous ski trip to the mountains. We loaded eight teens and four adults into a rented 15-passenger van and headed to the hills for the greatest five days of familying, feasting and skiing we've ever enjoyed.

Picture this. Husbands in the front seats, my beloved friend Jan, Brooklynne and I in the next row hidden behind a massive wall of snowboards and skis. Behind us two more rows of teenagers. Truly, my dear friend Jan is the First Lady of the Kitchen in our circle of friends. And that's a pretty big circle.

As soon as we pulled out of Regina, our husbands inquired about breakfast. Naturally. No problem, Jan had freshly made warm cinnamon buns for the team. And who'd like some homemade cream cheese icing on that melt-in-your-mouth cinnamon bun? Now that's hospitality on the go. We had such fun that week offering hospitality to our families and to one another.

What would God's idea of a perfect Family and Friends Feast look like in your life? Would you consider taking that question to the Lord in prayer? He could be waiting to show you how to love and possibly entertain some angels in your midst. Doesn't that make you smile? I just love Jesus.

I pray that the heart of hospitality that God has given us is a reflection of Christ in our lives that points our children and friends to Jesus. When our family has feasted together we've become more like friends. When we've feasted with friends, we've become more like family. We're so grateful to God for our Family and Friends Feasts, and the ultimate feast we'll have with Him one day. No restaurants- the banquet will have already been spread out for us; no grocery lists- all lists will have been wiped away; no need to clean up- that will have been taken care of by Christ. Let the feasting begin.

With all this talk of **treats and sweets**, I can't neglect sharing a recipe I've used many times on cold winter nights or for those spur-of-the-moment dessert emergencies. It's a melding of chocolate cake, chocolate pudding and hot chocolate. Prep time is less than 10 minutes and in well under an hour you can go from desperate for a dessert to culinary diva of decadence. It's a really good idea. Shall we?

Hot Chocolate and Cake- A Love Story

1 cup flour (you decide between whole wheat or white)
2 t. baking powder
3/4 cup brown sugar
1/2 t. salt
3 T. cocoa powder
2 t. vanilla
3/4 cup milk
2 T. melted butter
1/3 cup chopped walnuts or pecans (optional)

The Crown

3/4 cup brown sugar
1/2 cup cocoa powder
2 cups boiling water

Preheat oven to 350° F. In a medium bowl combine flour, baking powder, sugar, salt and cocoa powder. Mix together the vanilla, milk, butter and nuts. Add to dry ingredients and stir to form a stiff dough. Scrape this little party into a lightly buttered 8" round pan. Combine the crowning ingredients and carefully pour this over the batter and bake for 35-40 minutes. Mmm... serve warm with whipped cream or ice cream. Serves 4-6 depending....

My friend Jan, who I mentioned earlier, is coming over for breakfast tomorrow morning. A few minutes ago I got a *(gasp) I have an idea!* moment as I was cutting up some fruit for miniature smoothies. (I'm serving them in small green tea cups. How cute is that?) I love this idea. Jan doesn't know it, but I'm going to invite her to share her classic and rather regal, cinnamon bun recipe with us. I will set the mood. When she arrives in the morning, the forecasted temperature is a frightening -42° C. I'll get Ron to light a welcoming fire. The aroma of fresh brewed coffee will billow around her head and the sight of summer fruits will flirt with her frozen cheeks. After much feasting and coffee, I'll lay my request before her and if we are blessed, which I'm sure we will be, we'll have one of the best cinnamon bun recipes known to a woman and her kitchen.

It's now 9:32 a.m. It's -41° C. and Jan has just pulled into our driveway.

11:15 a.m. The Lord has caused His face to shine upon us.... and upon our kitchens. With Jan's permission, I've renamed these. We had a few giggles over some of the silly names I suggested, but we settled on this one because the recipe is sinfully easy to make. What Jan likes about them is the quick turn-around time from start to finish. Definitely not a daunting cinnamon bun recipe.

Behold...

Jan's Buns of Sin-namon

2 1/4 cups flour
1 T. yeast
1/4 cup sugar
1/2 t. salt
1 cup milk
1/4 cup melted butter
1 egg
3/4 cup whole wheat flour

The good, good, gooey part... 1/2 cup barely melted butter, blended with 1 cup brown sugar and 2 T. cinnamon

In a bowl or in your electric mixer, combine the flour, yeast, sugar and salt. Warm the milk in the melted butter. Make sure it's not too hot and then add the egg. Add this liquid to the dry ingredients and watch a delightful dough gently begin to form. Add the whole wheat flour and beat until you have a soft, squishy dough. Let the dough rest for 10 minutes while you prepare the gooey goodness.

On a floured surface roll the dough into an 8" x 12" rectangle. Smear the goo all over the dough and roll it up along the long side. Cut it into 12 pieces. Oh, yes we're almost there. With a grateful heart, place each little bun into a greased 9" x 13" pan. Cover it up and place it in a warm place for about 45 minutes. Then into a 350° F. oven they go for about 20-30 minutes. Ahh... the aroma.

These could very well be the best cinnamon buns I've ever eaten. I mean it. Because I enjoy different textures and surprises in my food, I want you to experience that same thrill. To the goo, you can add dried cherries, pecans, chopped dried apricots, or chopped almonds. Oh, Lord have mercy!

One more thing... please give this next idea a try. When we vacation in Clear Lake, Manitoba we always visit a homey breakfast place with a great outdoor patio. Almost every morning. They cut their cinnamon buns in half horizontally, then lightly butter and grill the cut sides until they're toasty brown. I have nothing more to add other than to say... may the peace of Christ be with you as you enjoy these.

Twenty-Nine

Pleasant and Sweet

**Proverbs 16:24 Pleasant words
are a honeycomb,
Sweet to the soul and healing to the bones.**

Pleasant

God knew I needed a pleasant little idea for the 14-hour road trip from Regina, Saskatchewan to Denver, Colorado.

We are past the days of fussy children, leaky juice boxes and sticky fingers that used to plague our car trips. Now our young adult children love to watch movies in the van and listen to their music. But I've learned the convenience of this commuter technology trumps good old-fashioned talking time, so I wanted an idea to stimulate some lively interaction on this journey.

When I pray, I do so in expectation, knowing that God is definitely going to do something. Even by doing what appears to us to be nothing, He's doing something in our lives. Sometimes what I consider to be the most insignificant prayers, are the ones that God answers in the most profound ways.

I'll be honest, a playful game for a car full of adults is not high on my priority list of prayers. But I've seen how God cares about even my smallest prayerful thoughts- the kind of fleeting thoughts that never really make it into my prayer time. Perhaps God responded to those thoughts that day so you could be encouraged today, but whatever His plan may have been, it happened- I gasped and exclaimed, "I have an idea!"

I pulled out a little book and began to jot down some odd questions. What is the official state beach in Texas? What city in Texas is known as "taco city"? Who can make the best pig squeal sound in the family? Where in Texas do they hold the annual blueberry festival? Who sang Rocky Mountain High? What does Colorado mean? Which child was the youngest in the family to get stitches and where were they? Which child was born with chubby arms? It was my Random Questions Trivia Game. I kept this idea to myself and planned to bring it out on the road trip at just the right time.

When I finally pulled out my little blue book, I began with my usual introduction, "one day a week or so ago I got an idea..." but I was drowned out with the usual moans and groans. That kind of reaction has never deterred me, because I know my family is secretly quite curious and willing. You may recall reading this in my introduction.

Amidst all the grumbling about my silly games, I could hear answers blurted out from all areas of the van. We laughed and saw that God cared enough to bless us with a sweet and pleasant time as a family. The Random Questions Trivia Game was easy to put together and came with no price tag. It's another good idea that will reappear on our next road trip.

I'm going to let you in on a secret. In 48 hours this book is off to the printer. I'm just doing a quick look through it one more time and as I read this chapter I'm gasping and getting an idea. In a couple of weeks we're headed to the lake for a family vacation. Ten people, five cooking teams (Chapter14!), one car, one truck, one van, 53 boxes of food, a truck full of towels, eight sets of golf clubs, bocce ball, horseshoes, a croquet set, six tennis racquets, five board games, four bikes, three old pool noodles, 10 faded lawn chairs and a good coffee maker. There is so much to prepare, but I've just decided I must make time to create a new Random Questions Trivia Game for the short road trip. I will make it in triplicate, one for each vehicle. The thought of this makes me tingle. I thank God that I never tire of a playful new idea.

Going on a road trip this summer? Plan ahead with your own version of the Random Questions Trivia Game. Perhaps there's someone in your family who'd be interested in making up the game for you? That makes a good idea even better.

And Sweet...

I needed one more sweet little idea to add to Genevieve's 21st birthday gift- some kind of special keepsake, something personal and practical. What would a darling young woman want from her parents that would make her say, "Oh that's so special, wow, what a great idea, I love it. I'll get lots of use out of this, thanks, I love you!"

Ladies, you know the kind of gift I'm talking about, not a costly one, but more of an "I thought of you" gift, as my friend Susan calls it. You can usually picture it in your mind and you know it's the perfect one the instant you spot it at a store. I know it's happened to you.

There were still a few weeks before I had to give this gift, so I really wasn't too concerned, but as I prepared dinner one night I got a little idea. I was flipping through my recipe file and my eyes widened, I sort of gasped and knew there was an idea brewing that had the potential of becoming something good.

Hmm... I decided I could give Genevieve a little collection of our favourite family recipes. Yes! I could put them on cute recipe cards and she'd have a taste of home in her own Texas kitchen. What a great idea, I thought as I began to search for special recipes that I knew she loved. Before long I had about a dozen winners, from appetizers to desserts. In my funny little head, I pictured these handwritten treasures bundled together with a pink ribbon and attached to her 21st birthday card. Simple enough.

But why, I ask you, do seemingly small, basic projects often turn into mammoth, out of control events of monumental proportions? This was a modest, straightforward plan, until I walked by that 75% off table at the mall. What was this? Adorable recipe boxes and coordinating cards all on sale, just for me? Hmm... still believing this would be a small-scale project, I purchased one package of cards and a recipe box.

By the time I got home I'd decided to add a few more recipes to the dozen I'd already chosen. I'm sure it doesn't surprise you to hear that I went through the first package of recipe cards in one night.

Now friends, the most handwriting I do is to quickly jot a little love note or thank you card now and then, so a full night of writing out recipes was a challenge. But even with an aching and cramped hand, I managed to drive myself to the store the next morning to pick up one more package of cards. While I was there I remembered we had three other children who would someday celebrate their 21st birthdays. Perhaps I should plan ahead for them. It was at that moment when the original, simple idea went from sweet to sweat. By the time I left the store I had three more recipe boxes, ten packages of recipe cards and hours of work ahead of me.

The dining room table became a processing center/ publishing house/culinary catalogue/ administrative hub for cards, recipes and boxes. I felt the need to set up barricades around the dining room to prevent anyone from breathing near my well-organized mess of recipes. There were piles of recipes to consider and to re-consider if space, time and my crippled right hand permitted. Please don't ask me why I was compelled to complete four recipe boxes in two weeks when I knew the other children were still years away from their 21st birthdays. You must've done something this ridiculous once, or even twice. Please tell me you have.

By the time her birthday arrived, Ron and I found ourselves in Comfort, Texas celebrating

Genevieve's special day. In our family, we get more excited about giving one another gifts, than receiving them and believe me, this was true once again. Today, seven years later, her recipe box has expanded with more recipes and is accented with splashes of butter and batter.

Since then, Alexandra and Jamison have turned 21 and I've handed out two more recipe boxes. What a thrill and relief it's been to have ready-made keepsake gifts to present to each of them. Months before Jamison's 21st birthday, he asked me if he'd be awarded a recipe box similar to his older sisters- I can't tell you how sweet that question was to my ears. Only one more box remains to be given, then all the children will have a taste of home in their kitchen, wherever that may be.

Girlfriend, let me ask you, what's the "recipe box" that the Lord is waiting to use in your family? You may find that God will use everyday things to show you the pleasant and sweet thoughts that are on His mind as you live your life in Him.

And one of the newest recipes in all the boxes is...

Christmas Cran-Baby Sauce

1 cup water
1 cup brown sugar
12 oz. fresh cranberries
1 small orange, peeled, seeded and pureed
1 apple, cored and chopped finely

1 ripe pear, cored and chopped finely
3/4 cup mixed dried fruit
1/4 cup dried cranberries
3/4 cup chopped nuts, choose your favourite, I use pecans
1 t. cinnamon
1/2 t. apple pie spice

Bring water and sugar to a boil for one minute. Reduce heat and add remaining ingredients. Cover and simmer gently for about 25-35 minutes or until the cranberries have gone snap, crackle, pop, and the sauce has thickened. Sample. Mmm... cool and store in canning jars for up to two weeks. Merry Christmas to you, my little sugar-plum!

Thirty

A Tacky Cardigan and Some Guacamole

Psalm 100 Shout joyfully to the LORD, all the earth. Serve the LORD with gladness; Come before Him with joyful singing. Know that the LORD Himself is God; It is He who has made us, and not we ourselves; We are His people and the sheep of His pasture. Enter His gates with thanksgiving And His courts with praise. Give thanks to Him, bless His name. For the LORD is good; His lovingkindness is everlasting And His faithfulness to all generations.

What do many Canadians do on Saturday nights in the winter, when the darkness sets in by 4:57 p.m., a day of errands has been satisfied, and all we want are our warm slippers and a cozy blanket?

Here are some hints to help you answer that question. My husband was born and raised in Montreal. On an outdoor rink. Now he has bad knees. When our son was only moments old, Ron talked to him about fishing and playing... you know what, in the winters together.

We consider ourselves average Canadians, so we do what I think many of us do on Saturday evenings- we invite some friends over for two and a half hours, set out some comfort food, put our feet up and watch Hockey Night in Canada. Hockey doesn't run in my blood like an end-to-end rush. I was a figure skater, I have no brothers and my father didn't play hockey, but when Ron and I got married it was a given that on Saturday nights we'd have friends over for casual food and serious hockey.

Without exception, we'd serve homemade pizza. It was a sacred event... pizza, friends and hockey. It all started in our cozy, 800 square foot apartment in downtown Calgary in the winter of 1978. You'll find that only a few things about our Saturday nights have changed in 30-ish years.

The changes: our numbers have tripled and so has the size of our home. Our bulky 1978 white flour pizza recipe has been replaced with a slender, thin crust whole wheat version, and toppings now feature pesto, feta, kalamata olives and shrimp, instead of the pepperoni and mush-rooms of our past.

The constants: the sun still sets by 5:00 p.m., Saturday errands still exist, and living on the prairies, I find I cling to my toasty slippers and quilted blanket tighter than ever. Hockey still comes on at 6:00 p.m. Together in the kitchen, Ron and I still prepare and serve to anyone who is around, our 30-year-old tradition of Hockey Night in Canada Pizza.

You see friends, I felt then, as I feel now, that we couldn't serve pizza every Saturday night to our friends without calling it something more than just pizza. So I named it our Hockey Night in Canada Pizza and that title has stuck. (Tomorrow night we'll be serving it around 7:00 p.m. so if you're around, you're welcome to join us.) Even three decades ago I had these *(gasp) I have an idea!* episodes in my life.

I've always had a desire to create a theme for most of our social times with family or friends. My earliest recollection of my attraction to themed events is the trousseau tea my mother had planned for me a week prior to our wedding day. I don't recall being a bridezilla. But I must have had a *(gasp) I have an idea!* moment in the spring of 1978 because I clearly remember wanting a tea party immersed in pink. Rewind with me to the '70s. There were dainty pink sandwiches, strawberry punch, pink squares and pink décor everywhere you looked in my parent's elegant home. Everything we ate and drank had to be a shade of pink. And there I was in my soft pink cotton dress with a drawstring waist and delicate cap sleeves. Bless my mother who graciously pulled the whole beautiful pink thing together for me.

A few years later came life in the Stampede City. More gasping. More ideas. We made it an annual practice to attend the Calgary Stampede Parade and then invite everyone we knew for a barbeque brunch. It was held on the back deck of our home where we served a traditional Calgary Stampede breakfast right off the barbeque. Pancakes, sausages, baked beans and lots of coffee. Because it was the kick-off for Stampede week, our guests were required to come in western wear. It was Calgary, it worked.

Take Valentine's Day. When the children were little I wanted to show them we needed to celebrate God's love, so we'd have an annual Valentine's Day party at our home. It was usually on a Saturday afternoon and, you guessed it, we'd all wear red, eat red, drink red, do red crafts and paint red hearts on our cheeks. I recall wearing a very tacky pink and red cardigan with hearts all over it. It was the late '80s and early '90s! Some of you gals know exactly what I'm talking about. I'm getting a flashback of oversized shoulder pads too. At the time, the seasonal cardigan theme was a huge hit with the children. I had one for every season. Some seasonal clothing works. This wardrobe did not. Thankfully they made me retire them all a few years ago. Remember things I'm thankful for... Chapter 13?

The children grew up too quickly and I found myself planning high school graduation parties. For both Genevieve and Alexandra we had formal sit down dinners. We transformed the dining room of our home into an elegant candle lit setting for 12 with dinner served by Ron and me. I was overjoyed when I got a *(gasp) I have an idea!* moment for the theme of Genevieve's dinner. I called it A Night to Remember. The two highlights of the evening involved fire. The first was Ron's tableside flambéed cherry crepes. Fabulous. The second was when Genevieve's friend, Janelle, set her serviette on fire during dinner. Frantic. Truly a night to remember.

Themed dinners continued. After much consultation with the Lord one spring, Genevieve decided to attend Bible school in Texas. I remember thinking this was cause for celebration. And then I had an idea, a Texas Fiesta! Our dear friends Elwood and Lorraine, who have deep Texas ties, were happy to share their Texas paraphernalia and décor with us. I decorated using their flags, tablecloth and lone star treasures. They joined us as we barbequed some big fat steaks and surprised our soon-to-be southern sweetheart with a Texas feast on the Canadian prairies.

It was our way of honouring God for His faithfulness in her life and for leading her to this decision. The night we held that Texas barbeque in our backyard, God, in His sovereignty, knew the plans He had not only for her, but also for each of our other children to attend His Hill Bible School over the coming years. Even Ron and I have attended Bible school on and off over the past 10 years. God bless Texas! It's become our second home.

New Year's Eve celebrations aren't a really big deal to Ron and me- it's simply another opportunity for a relaxing get together in our home with friends over the holidays. As I planned one New Year's Eve gathering, God gave me a gaspingly good idea for a theme. Naturally, food was the first item on the list of must-haves at the party.

Because our friends are gracious guests, most of them wanted to bring food to share. My response to their kind offers was this- if they came bearing gifts of food, it had to begin with the same letter as their last name. For example, the Hansons brought hummus. The Armstrongs brought antipasto and crackers. We, the Gladyszs, made guacamole. What a great night of fellowship we had around the fire during our Name that Appetizer Night. Don't you love that idea? I love our friends. I really do.

So why Psalm 100? My study Bible shows me that each Psalm has a theme. Some of those themes are- songs of praise to God, the power of God, forgiveness because of God, confession to God, thankfulness to God and trust in God. It's always about Him. The book of Psalms is found at the center of the Bible, just as Christ is to be the center of our lives. I can go to God through the Psalms with any emotion or situation I face knowing I'll come face to face with Christ.

- Psalms about God's goodness- 29 & 96
- Psalms of praise- 8, 103 & 107
- Psalm of forgiveness- 51
- Psalms for troubled times- 3, 42 & 46
- Psalm about raising a family- 127
- And Psalm 100- a Psalm of thanksgiving- all men are exhorted to praise God!

If God does themes, then so do I. But somewhere between the tacky cardigan and the guacamole, God has shown me the need to display the theme of Christ in my life.

The cowboy hats now collect dust on the shelf, the face paints have dried up and cold pizza is not all it's cracked up to be. But God is always Lord. Verse five in Psalm 100 tells us... "For the LORD is good; His lovingkindness is everlasting and His faithfulness to all generations."

Hockey Night in Canada Pizza

Whole Wheat Pizza Dough

1 cup warm water
2 T. honey
2 1/4 t. yeast (one package)
1/4 cup extra virgin olive oil
3 cups flour, half white and half whole wheat
1 t. sea salt

Prepare the dough your favourite way. We roll this dough recipe into one 16" round for two delicious reasons. Firstly, we prefer a thin crust pizza to the big fat one-incher we made back in the 70's. Secondly, because we often have leftover pizza to freeze and enjoy on a whim another day. You can also roll your dough into a rectangle and bake it on a cookie sheet. A rectangular pizza gives you some nice gooey, crustless middle pieces.

The Top Toppings of 2011- pesto, feta, kalamata olives, shrimp, sun-dried tomatoes, red peppers. Lots of captivating colours, lots of bold flavours.

Bake at 400° F. for about 15 minutes. Squeeze a little fresh lemon juice over the top of the shrimp before serving!

Thirty-One

iCraft

Psalm 128:3 Your wife shall be like a fruitful vine within your house, Your children like olive plants Around your table.

This book was pretty much done, or so I thought. But a few days before it was on its way to the publisher, the Lord opened my eyes to two very significant ideas He orchestrated years ago around our kitchen table. I began to struggle with the thought of adding another chapter, not because I didn't want to write. I love to write. But it meant I'd have a total of 33 chapters. For some reason I thought 33 was an awkward number of chapters for the book. Thirty-two seemed more balanced or something. After a few days, God made it clear we'd be having 33 chapters. (I'm the one who was off balance.) Then He put an exclamation mark on His decision by reminding me that 33 is a very significant kingdom number. It's commonly agreed upon by biblical scholars that Jesus lived for 33 years. Enough said.

It's 2011. Even though some of us may not be very technologically savvy, you and I both know it's the era of iStuff. Phones, pods and pads.

As I've already mentioned, we raised our children on Jesus, and crafts. Not iStuff. So here's what I've been thinking about lately. Is there any room in life for good old-fashioned crafts? I wonder if it's time for you to gather around the kitchen table with your children for an afternoon of crafts? Call it iCrafts if that's more appealing to your children!

Ron and I recently had a lot of fun together doing a mini renovation of our kitchen. I lovingly called it Renos by Ron. You've heard me refer to our kitchen as command central of our home. It's my haven and my comfort zone. I love it. One of my favourite new touches is the wall art above the large window by the kitchen table. Our friend Sheena made the word "Gather" for us out of bronze vinyl. When I look up at the word "Gather" it causes me to become nostalgic, reminiscent and very thankful.

For 30 years God has gathered our family together around our big, oak, kitchen table where He's graciously provided us with so much more than just meals. That table has seen fabric paint projects, scrapbooking escapades, colouring contests, Easter egg decorating disasters, gingerbread house sculpting, wreath making, Christmas crafts, sewing debacles and the Cross-stitch Club.

Let me tell you about the Cross-stitch Club which began in the days before phones, pods and pads. It was an era when I cross-stitched anything I could get my hands on. Aprons, tea towels, ornaments, quilts, dresses, baby bibs and bonnets. Here's where you may begin to think I'm old fashioned. One of the best parts of my cross-stitch crazy years is my vivid memory of teaching all four of our children to cross-stitch. I even have a little ornament tucked away that Jamison made for me when he was a preschooler. It's pink and mauve. Sorry Jamison.

But 20 years ago God took our simple stitches and crossed them over into our neighbourhood. It started out as an ordinary Friday. Genevieve invited a few girls over to play after school, but after devouring some snacks, they picked up some cross-stitch materials I had sitting around and began asking me questions. Little 10-year-old girls wanted to learn about cross-stitching. Glory! Hallelujah! (You've now read 30 some odd chapters of this book and know me fairly well. I was in my glory.) We gathered around the kitchen table and stitched.

The following Friday the same thing happened, but this time a few more girls came over. We snacked and cross-stitched together. By the third week we had so many little ladies that we relocated to the family room. I moved from girl to girl, answering questions, untying knots, undoing errors and rethreading needles.

It must have been one Friday morning as I was anticipating my after school visitors, that I gasped and exclaimed to myself, "I have an idea!" So when those sweet young gals burst into the house at 3:30 p.m. I officially welcomed them to the Cross-stitch Club. This went on for the whole school year. Themes. Love them.

The Lord has caused me to remember so many pleasant moments from our Fridays together. My favourite stories involve popcorn, the local church and a pair of scissors.

I decided the snack of choice would be very simple at our Cross-stitch Club. Popcorn and water. Easy to make, easy to clean up. Each Friday, God used one particular girl to remind me that a home can be a wonderful venue to show His love in our community. With the aroma of freshly popped popcorn in the air, this girl would run into the family room and tell me our home felt so welcoming and smelled good. I knew she spent a lot of time on her own after school and on weekends. This little lady was by far the best cross-stitcher in the group and her handiwork was far better than mine. Each week God emphasized to me the importance of using our home for Him.

When the members of our Cross-stitch Club heard there was a children's club program at our church that included a craft time, many of the girls joined us there on Wednesday nights. And, my friends, you know that intermingled with crafts, gym time and snacks, those little ladies also heard all about the life of Christ and the life they could have in Christ. Several of them gave their lives to Jesus. Glory to God in the highest!

Then there was scissor-girl. Alexandra and Jamison, who were able little stitchers, were allowed to join in with Genevieve's friends, but what about Brooklynne who was only about three-years-old? Genevieve's friends, who loved Brooklynne, gave her the title and job of being scissor-girl. She was in her glory, hanging around her big sister's friends and fulfilling the vital role of thread snipper. One day I noticed she had her scissors hanging from a tiny hole in her tee-shirt. I asked her about it. She told me she'd cut a slit in her shirt and slipped the scissors in, so she always had them handy. How could I be angry? She had the gift of administration and creativity at a very early age! Yes, dangerous, I know.

A few days ago Ron and I attended a banquet for the children's club program I just told you about. This is a ministry that God is using mightily for His kingdom. The speaker, Jerry Durston, said something that God has etched in my mind. He explained that the motto for their program is, "to develop hearts that desire to please God." Oh girl-friends, if we all had that purpose in us! Hearts that desire to please God.

Jerry and his gracious wife, Sharon are dear friends of ours. He's the founder of Club DJ and also the Provincial Director of Child Evangelism Fellowship of Saskatchewan. Please find out more at *www.clubdj.ca* and *www.cefsask.org.*

Pompoms and Performances

When I was very pregnant with Brooklynne, I did a weird thing. (Call it hormones.) I gave six-year-old Genevieve and four-year-old Alexandra my permission to start a home business. (Hormones.) Those two little ladies began a small, rather too successful, cottage industry called Pompom Animals. It was one of those moments when I said, "sure we can do this." And within a few days was way in over my head. Who would've thought Pompom Animals would have taken off like it did? A bag of pompoms, pencils, some googly eyes and a hot glue gun.

We took orders from their classmates for small, medium or large pompom animals, glued onto the end of a pencil. That was it my friends. Once again, our kitchen table turned into one big production center. My fingers were blistered from little burns. Back then there was no such thing as a low temperature glue gun. We sold embellished pencils for an insignificant amount of money and probably didn't get paid for most of the panda bears, kittens, puppies, rabbits, penguins and teddy bears we pumped out. But God had us gather around the kitchen table with laughter as He made our home lively and alive in Christ.

Make yourself a cup of tea and get comfortable because I want to share one of the best *(gasp) I have an idea!* moments ever. I know I've said that before too. But I'm overwhelmed with the goodness God's shown us as our family has gathered around the kitchen table.

Have you ever met a family you love so much that you wish you were really and truly related to them? That's how we felt when we met our friends Ron and Marlene and their two girls. During the elementary school years, their girls spent many hours playing in our home and preparing Dance and Sing for Fun.

Dance and Sing for Fun. That phrase always brings a smile to my face. Genevieve, Alexandra, Jamison, Brooklynne, Janelle and Whitney would enjoy a snack at the kitchen table after school, then head downstairs to rehearse. These were all children who were involved in voice, dance or music lessons. They were also very fond of crafts. Combine those gifts with a couple of older sisters with budding leadership skills, and the outcome was Dance and Sing For Fun.

This was a production, and I do mean production, that the six children would put on for us after many, many intense hours of planning and rehearsing. There were group and individual numbers, singing and dancing. Extravagant backdrops that often really did drop! As the only adult at home after school, I had the privilege of hearing everything that went on in our basement during those daily rehearsals. A lot of laughter, some tears, a bit of complaining and accusations of bossiness. Personalities emerged and so did some great music. Dances were perfected and menus were planned. These young children also learned that social events involve food.

When performance night arrived, Ron and Marlene, as well as my husband and I were the only honoured guests in attendance. We headed downstairs and were met by Jamison, who was always put in charge of ticket taking. The girls had him dressed in a velvet costume and set up with a toy cash register, to collect the one-dollar admission price. Dance and Sing for Fun lasted about two hours with a short intermission, during which time we were also required to purchase the refreshments Marlene and I had prepared earlier in the day. This still makes me laugh. Over the years the children organized five or six nights of talent for us. We were blessed parents.

But as I reminisced over this idea, God showed me some interesting things.

Jamison, a singer/songwriter, is currently finishing recording a debut full-length solo album. Listen at *www.jamisontroy.com*.

Alexandra has a lovely blog where she posts inspirations to finding joy in cooking, crafting, entertaining, styling, writing and sharing. Please find her blog, Alexandra's Joys, at *alexandrasjoys.blogspot.com*. This is how creative she is... her full name is Alexandra Joy.

Genevieve and Brooklynne are innovative crafters and bakers extraordinaire. Some of their favourite past-times? Making hand-made cards, accessories and home décor, and baking.

Janelle is actively involved in our community as a high school cheerleading coach and Whitney is now a stunning professional dancer.

You've heard people say that God cares about the details in our lives. But after rereading Psalm 128:3, I believe He also cares about His life in our details. Details that happen around your table... from googly eyes to giggling girls.

I've come to realize that kitchen table ministry is alive and well in my world. This morning God lovingly reminded me that He ministered to me a long time ago at a kitchen table. When I was in my early 20s I knelt beside the kitchen table in my friend Sherry's home and invited Christ into my life to be my Lord and Saviour. Yes, kitchen tables will always be a special, sacred place for me.

Never underestimate what God can do as you gather around your kitchen table with your children. What He prompts you to do today could have lifelong kingdom results. For a few hours, would you put away the iStuff... phones, pods and pads in your home and take a chance on the old-fashioned? Like the iCraft of 2011.

Thirty-Two

Freedom 51

Philippians 2:13 ... for it is God who is at work in you, both to will and to work for His good pleasure.

I really dislike the phrase "empty nest." To me, it sounds like a lonely and lifeless place. I've always pictured a carefully made robin's nest, once filled with chirping little hungry birds, protective parents and fat worms, now sitting abandoned and void of any signs of life or love. Empty nest...boo.

Many of our friends, whose children had grown up and left home, talked about their lives as empty nesters with delight. Although this sounded like freedom, joy and a new-found life, there was still something about the phrase, empty nest or worse yet, empty nesters, that made me want to cry. Please hear what I'm saying. It wasn't the stage that troubled me, it was the term.

In His infinite goodness, God saw my quivering heart, so as we approached this new stage, He graciously placed wise and mature empty nesters, who were alive in Christ, across our path. We could see that life could be rich and fulfilling at this point too, because of Jesus at work in them for His pleasure.

We could see it coming. One summer our well-meaning friends kept reminding us that by the fall of 2008 we'd be empty nesters. Although that was true, how was I going to avoid this label? Could I interrupt Jamison's plan to move to Calgary? Or keep Brooklynne from heading south to Bible school simply to avoid being called an empty nester? I knew what September would mean, but still I refused to succumb to being called an... empty nester.

Then, in a matter of a few days, it all happened. We drove Brooklynne to school in Texas and immediately after returning home, we repacked the van with reptiles and recording equipment, bikes and boxes, and our very enthusiastic son. We pointed the vehicle west and headed to Calgary.

Twenty-four hours later, I sat still before the Lord on the quiet eight-hour drive back home. For a moment, emptiness and vulnerability began to creep in. But God immediately stirred, inviting me to trust Him to turn what I thought was sudden poverty, into fruitfulness. And to believe Him to take my deserted little nest and transform it into an abundant life. Because He was still at work in me for His good pleasure. When we finally turned the corner onto our street, Jesus had turned my heart towards Himself in a new fresh way. I believed He was my only hope in this new stage of life.

There Ron and I were, just the two of us, with four empty bedrooms and 25 years of parenting on our resumes. Now what? He muttered something about being empty nesters. I pretended I hadn't heard that. But I think it was when he dared to bring up the empty nest thing for a second time, that I burst out, "No way, we're not empty nesters! This is Freedom 51!"

The poor man. He had no idea what I was talking about, and to be perfectly honest, neither did I at first. But then I quickly realized the Lord had handed me the gift of a *(gasp) I have an idea!* moment, that He would go on to use for His good pleasure throughout the coming months and years. This was new freedom because of Christ. And since I was 51 years old when this all occurred, it made complete sense to me that this time should be called, "Freedom 51."

Over the next few months God showed me how I now had fewer distractions in my home and life. Christ alone could be my distraction any time of the day. It was easier for me to be the helper suitable for my husband- just as God originally intended! I was freer to live out some of the *one anothers* that God talks about in His Word- to offer hospitality, comfort, build up, encourage, spur on, bear with, serve and rejoice with so many of the women in my life. My time with Him, in His Word and in prayer, became more alive and richer than ever. God showed me it's good to be distracted- firstly by Him and then by the things that He has determined to be of value for His kingdom and for His glory.

What a glorious gift! What a great idea He had with Freedom 51! Although Ron and I miss our four children with a passion, we've delighted in being a family of two again, returning to what God established in 1978. For this new season, with all its unknowns, we asked Christ to be our joy and strength. So dear friend, I proclaim to you, that it was only by His utmost grace that we survived, grew and rejoiced in that first year of Freedom 51.

Although Ron is still busy running our two restaurants, Freedom 51 allows us to...

- have coffee together most mornings before he goes to work... (For 25 years, mornings were all about getting children to school on time.)
- try to get to the gym together several times a week... (Although running after toddlers can seem like a workout.)
- enjoy dinner where and when and how we feel like it... (Poof! the crazy nightly circuit of non-stop activities has disappeared.)
- meet our friends (who still choose to call themselves empty nesters) for coffee in the evening... (Unheard of prior to this.)
- golf together on nice summer mornings... (Sometimes I pretend to wave at imaginary fans cheering as I step up to the ball.)
- enjoy dinner at my Mom's... (She loves to cook great Greek food for us every Sunday.)
- have late lunches together at the restaurant to discuss business matters... (Over the years, my afternoon discussions were mostly directed towards toddlers as I promoted the benefits of long naps.)
- plan getaways to see the children... (Three cheers for airline reward points!)

- meet with four other couples for Bible study, prayer and fabulous food on Friday nights... (No need to worry about babysitters or driving children from point A to point B.)
- pray together...

But one of our most cherished times that God initiated during our first year of Freedom 51 is our discipleship group or "d-group," an idea we copied from His Hill Bible School. Each Friday morning a staff member at the school gathers with a few students to discuss a book and pray. Breakfast is a must.

The idea of having our own d-group began one morning shortly after Freedom 51 began. I looked at Ron across the breakfast table and gasped, "I have an idea." He looked at me questioningly over the top of his coffee mug. With great enthusiasm I explained that we could have our own Friday morning d-group-for-two and read the same book as the students at Bible school. After all, we still had two children there.

I've tossed many outrageous ideas at my patient husband, but our d-group was one idea that Ron agreed to without hesitation. We took turns making breakfast, and then settled into our sunny family room to discuss a book over many cups of good coffee.

After reading a few different d-group books, we changed things up a bit and listened online to our good friend, Charlie McCall, who is the Director of His Hill, preach a series of messages on the book of Revelation.

God met us each Friday morning as we knelt before Him praying for our children and their future spouses. Those prayers expanded to include their mission trips and pleasure trips, business ventures and roommate adventures, vision and provision for our children. One morning Ron prayed for "Boazian suitors" for our daughters. That made me chuckle a wee bit.

Here are a couple of ideas. You could visit our church in Texas, Boerne Bible Church, where Charlie preaches, without ever leaving your home. One morning, put on a pot of coffee, grab your Bible and listen at *www.boernebiblechurch. org.* Or you can pretend go to His Hill Bible School by listening to classes online from the comfort of your own home. Find this jewel at *www.hishill. org.* You could have your own d-group!

Some of my ideas have been around for decades and some, like Freedom 51, are brand new. Old or new, I'm thrilled to be involved wherever the Lord is active. And, oh how I pray for many more exciting Freedom 51 years of God ordained, God at work, and God glorifying times that Ron and I will share together.

Although Ron never serves this for breakfast at our d-group, he often makes it for dinner. Each time it gets better. I decided that this would be his signature dish! So I had to include it for you my friend. Join me as Ron escorts us through this outrageously delicious dish I call...

My oh my, that's Great Thai!

Before we begin, I need you to imagine you're building a three-tiered dish. There will be the jasmine rice layer as your foundation. This fragrant, nutty rice is popular in Asian cooking and has a rich aroma. Continue building your dish with colourful veggies and a protein. Finally you'll have the opportunity to get sassy with a Thai sauce of heat meets sweet.

So, let's get started. Prepare your sauce by combining...

2 T. of red chili paste (we use Sambal Oelek)
4 T. of brown sugar
1 cup coconut milk (use premium, not light)
You can adjust the amounts of these ingredients to suit your taste.

Heat this mixture up slightly and set it aside.

Prepare your jasmine rice according to the directions on the package.

Since you're the cook, you get to select your favourite veggies and cut them into bite size pieces. We use red and green peppers, broccoli, grape tomatoes, garlic, bok choy, red onions, water chestnuts, green onions and zucchini. Stir fry the veggies in a little sesame oil until they're softened and you see the colours become more vibrant. Set this aside and keep it warm.

More choices. Decide upon your protein. Do you feel like chicken, beef or perhaps some seafood? Our favourite is shrimp and scallops. Once that big and delicious decision is made, stir fry it in some sesame oil until it's thoroughly cooked.

Now the fun part. Add the veggies and sauce to your protein and heat the whole mixture until it barely begins to bubble. Place your rice in a bowl, spoon a generous helping of your amazing culinary creation over the steaming rice and garnish it with some fresh, chopped cilantro or parsley.

This smells so incredible, you won't even have to call them for dinner. My oh my!

Thirty-Three

Treat of the Day Bag

**Proverbs 24:3 & 4 By wisdom a house is built,
And by understanding it is established;
And by knowledge the rooms are filled
With all precious and pleasant riches.**

Writing this book with Jesus has been an epic journey. He's taken my hand and we've meandered through lavish moments laden with His love. God has blessed me and met me every single day along the way, using Ron and our children as instruments of inspiration and encouragement.

Even very recently, Genevieve and Alexandra suggested I include another much loved idea from their childhood. Keep reading and you'll see why it's a winner. I'm amazed how God takes what we think is a simple little gesture and turns it into precious and pleasant riches.

That's what happened back in 1980-something as I was getting children and diapers and toys and car snacks and drinks and a few other

necessities ready for a road trip to visit my parents. They lived about three hours from us. I
was planning a little one-week getaway to their
home for some quality family time. My dad and
mom were the kind of grandparents who dropped
everything for their grandchildren. Time with my
parents meant homemade ice cream, gardening,
strolling through Chinatown, baking pies, violin
recitals and backyard barbeques.

A few days before we headed out on our road
trip I began to think about what kind of small
thank you gift I should take to my mom. Certainly
not necessary, but I wanted a special treat to give
her for hosting us. My sweet friend, you know
what happened next. God bestowed upon me a
most generous *(gasp) I have an idea!* moment,
one that sent me running to make a list. I love a
good list.

My list read: pretty gift bag, serviettes, candles, note paper and homemade granola. A few
hours later I added banana oat squares, bubble
bath and photos to the list. This idea was coming
together beautifully.

The next item on the list was to find a gift bag.
I can vividly picture the one I purchased for my
mother. It became the first and most cherished
Treat of the Day Bag. I chose a bag with a delicate
pattern of cheery pink roses- my mother's favourite flower. God showed me that during my visit
He was going to bless her with a daily treasure
from the Treat of the Day Bag.

I remember exactly how it went. The morning
after we arrived, with the aroma of sizzling pancakes wafting up to my bedroom, I headed down
to breakfast with my rosy, pink Treat of the Day

Bag. Smiling inside and out, I placed it on the kitchen table, and said something like, "Mom, I have a little treat for you." She giggled and thanked me in an oh-you-shouldn't-have tone. Ahh... lovely serviettes. I quietly returned the gift bag to my room.

The next morning. Candles.

The next morning. Photos of the children.

The next morning. Granola.

And so on for the rest of the week. Each morning I'd let one of the children choose a goodie from my suitcase for the Treat of the Day Bag for their Yiayia, (that's grandmother in Greek). I could sense that Mom looked forward to a little something that said, "you're wonderful, thank you for having us and we love you."

Time passed.

Another road trip to Dad and Mom's. Another list of potential items for the Treat of the Day Bag. More smiles, more thanks and more I love yous. Same pink gift bag. It became an icon and essential item on each trip to Yiayia's house. We used and reused that well-worn gift bag for a decade!

More time passed and our children moved to far-away places. One glorious day I found myself booking a flight to see our daughters who lived in the Texas Hill Country. God gave me a magnificent idea for my hostess, Genevieve- a Treat of the Day Bag. She was very surprised and delighted when she received her goodies each morning. A special bag traveled with Ron last winter when he went to spend a week of guy time with Jamison in Vancouver. I set him up with a gift bag of granola, shampoo, tea, muffins and love notes from home.

My friend, there is something warming to my heart when I plan a trip to see any of our children. Included in my preparations is always a collection of little pleasures to present daily in a special bag. I know the children look back at that 1980s gift bag and see how Jesus used a few candles and some squares to create a family tradition and avenue for showing love towards one another.

Last summer Ron and I visited our friends Bill and Wendy in Winnipeg. The men went fishing while Wendy and I strolled through some unique collectable shops and lush gardens. Because our friends have a Texas connection, their Treat of the Day Bag consisted of a bottle of our favourite southern barbeque sauce, Texas salsa, a jar of jalapeños and a candle made in the Lone Star State. Friends or family, Treat of the Day Bags are a gesture of love and thanks.

I'm not exaggerating when I say that I bake, craft, sew or shop for weeks leading up to a Treat of the Day Bag event. I have a box set aside specifically for treats I purchase or make, knowing that someday God will use them in a holy way. Whenever I can, I exercise the Treat of the Day Bag ministry.

God's taken the pink rose buds from that first gift bag and caused His idea to blossom into another generation of Treat of the Day Bag givers. I delight in seeing how Christ has grown each of our children into thoughtful and gracious givers. The joy that God's given them is so apparent in their lives as they "treat" our family and their friends in tangible little ways.

Some Treat of the Day Bag ideas for you!

- baking... any kind of cookies, banana oat squares, muffins, cheese buns, homemade granola or Bev's Breakfast Beauties from Chapter 22
- crafting... a variety of pretty craft supplies such as buttons, ribbon and stickers for your friend to make her own cards
- loving... a collection of personal, hand written notes that you place in the Treat of the Day Bag daily... tell your friend why she is so special to you
- freshening... candles, sachets, flowers, perfume samples
- reading... a magazine, newsletter or a book from your library that God has used in your life
- cooking... write out some of your favourite recipes on attractive cards and include a few ingredients
- relaxing... bubble bath, lotion, soap, scrubs and bath salts
- hostessing... serviettes, candles, flowers from your garden, spices, herbs, or an apron
- praying... commit to pray for your friend regarding a particular need in her life.. write Bible verses on little cards for her
- photographing... baby, wedding, holiday, vacation- whatever you have that could be special to your friend, pictures speak the words we can't express
- wedding... a bride-to-be treat bag can include jewelry cleaner for the sparkle on her left

hand, nail polish, a ceramic ring dish and some hand lotion

I could go on and on. But that's enough from me today. I encourage you to sit down with the Lord and listen to Him regarding your giving. God has shown me how He can take the simple things in life that I place in a Treat of the Day Bag and turn them into precious and pleasant riches. Girls, as you fill your little treat bags, remember to ask God to fill your heart with wisdom and understanding and knowledge.

Head to the kitchen with me! Let's make some banana oat squares and granola. I've been making this recipe for banana oat squares for 25 years. The only thing that I've changed from time to time is what I call the mix-ins.

I Sing for Joy Banana Oat Squares

For the mix-ins I love to add any combination of fresh blueberries, walnuts, pecans, almonds, coconut, dried cranberries, chopped dried apricots or chocolate chips. Experiment for yourself. Be daring. Let me know what culinary adventure you go on with these squares. Make these a part of your kitchen table ministry.

5 T. softened butter
1 T. coconut oil

1/2 cup brown sugar
1 egg
1/4 t. salt
3 mashed bananas
2 cups oatmeal
1 cup or so of the mix-ins

Combine the butter, oil and sugar in a bowl and beat until smooth. Add the egg and the remaining ingredients, including your favourite mix-ins. Tell them they are the chosen ones. Place the batter into a greased 8" x 8" square pan and bake it at 350° F. for about 45 minutes. Cool and cut into squares. Eat one or two, then watch your family devour these gems. And yes, they will freeze. I sing for joy!

Oh là là Granola!

3 cups oatmeal
1 cup toasted coconut, the long fancy kind
1 cup wheat germ
1/2 cup sesame seeds
1 cup chopped almonds, pecans or walnuts... you choose!
1/2 cup pumpkin seeds
1/2 cup sunflower seeds

I've said it before, but I'll say it one more time. Girls, this is another easy recipe. Combine all of the ingredients in a large roasting pan. Then drizzle the granola with a silky blend of ...

3/4 cup melted butter

1/4 cup coconut oil (this adds such a burst of flavour!)

1/2 cup or so of maple syrup, the sweetness level is up to you

1 t. vanilla

1 T. cinnamon or pumpkin pie spice

Stir well and bake this lusciousness for about 30 minutes at 350° F. Stir it a few times and if you want you can add more of the melted butter mixture. Cool and store it in an airtight container for up to a month. It'll be gone before then.

What else do I do with a container of homemade granola from my pantry?

- Layer it with fruit and yogurt to make a breakfast parfait.
- I use granola to make fruit crisps. Choose seasonal fresh fruit and make a crisp as you normally would. For the topping use two cups of this granola mixed with about 3/4 cup or so of melted butter. Pack it in on top of your fruit and bake. In the autumn I use apples, pears, plums and walnuts to make a Fall Fruit Breakfast Crisp that I take as a unique brunch offering to our ladies' Bible study each September!
- Make barkola!

Barkola

Let's take a minute to revisit the recipe for Candy Cane Bark with a Bite in Chapter 6. On this fine day we're going to combine bark and granola to make... barkola! All we have to do is switch the mix-ins from the Candy Cane Bark recipe and replace them with some Oh là là Granola. Use white, dark or milk chocolate. You're not going to believe how magnificent this is.

For an added touch in the presentation, grease the inside of cookie cutters, (bells and trees at Christmas, hearts on Valentine's Day) place them on a parchment paper lined baking sheet and pour your chocolate into the cookie cutters. Sprinkle on the granola, chill until hardened, then very carefully pop the bark out of the mold. Serve a chunk of barkola with strawberry ice cream pie, Dreamy Creamy Cream Puffs, raspberry-banana crepes or the time-honoured classic- banana split. Jesus loves me, this I know!

I thank God for this collection of playful little stories focused on His ideas for our family that have helped to make our home lively and alive in Christ. I'm grateful for the gift of His presence in our lives and in our home. It is with great anticipation and reverence that I wait for Him to fill our home with more of His precious and pleasant riches in His perfect time! For I am reminded daily that it is...

By wisdom a house is built, and by understanding it is established; and by knowledge the rooms are filled with all precious and pleasant riches. Proverbs 24: 3 & 4

Dessert Time

Most authors call this portion of the book, the epilogue. But I prefer Dessert Time. Doesn't that sound so much more appealing? I want to give you a whimsical glimpse of how I've viewed this book.

I love cream puffs. Who doesn't? I don't eat them very often, but when I do get a chance- oh sister! Would you join me as we look at this book... as a cream puff?

Cream puffs are small, puffy, delicate little morsels of baked choux pastry. They're inviting to anyone who needs a little extra loving in their day. Cream puffs are usually filled with whipped cream or sweet custard. They're a very approachable dessert, not overpowering or excessively rich. You can eat one, or sit down with a plateful.

A cream puff begins as an empty, hollow shell. Rather inadequate and incomplete. If the baker stopped there, the most important element would be absent. There's a luscious, sweet filling waiting to be injected into that empty space which will cause the shell to overflow with life. Once the sweetness is nestled into that void, the cream puff comes alive and is finally complete.

This book was filled with playful ideas, heart-warming stories and treasured family recipes. But on its own it was incomplete and missing something. It needed to be made complete with the presence of the living God, through His life giving Word, or otherwise it was just a hollow shell. It is His sweetness breathed into a shell of a book that made it whole.

Oh dear friend, we are like an empty shell until Christ fills us with His sweet Spirit. Don't settle for half-baked and incomplete fare. Ask the God of all hope to fill you with His life and you will be complete in Him.

Naturally, I have to leave you with one final recipe! Please remember Jesus with every bite you take!

Dreamy Creamy Cream Puffs

At this very moment, as I type this, I'm sitting in the sunshine of my mother's inviting kitchen getting a lesson in the art of making the perfect cream puff. She's using a recipe dated 1970. This one is tried and true. She says so and I believe her. She's my mother.

1/2 cup butter
1 cup boiling water
1 cup sifted all purpose flour
1/4 t. salt
4 eggs
whipped cream

Try making some flavoured whipped cream for your cream puffs by folding in one of the following darlings. Finely crushed candy canes, lemon zest, cocoa powder or a mixture of espresso and brown sugar.

Mom takes this very seriously. She says to melt the butter in the boiling water. Add the flour and salt all at once and stir vigorously. She mentioned that a few times. We're getting an upper body workout while baking. Don't you love it? Cook and stir the mixture until it magically forms a ball, then take it off the heat and cool for a few minutes.

Get yourself a cold drink of water because you still have a bit of a workout left. Add the eggs, one at a time, beating each one until the dough is smooth. Work those arms ladies. I'm remembering what God says about the Proverbs 31 gal in verse 17. "She girds herself with strength and makes her arms strong." That's us.

Preheat the oven to 400° F. Butter or line your cookie sheet with parchment paper. Plop a heaping tablespoonful of silky, heavenly dough about 3 inches apart in which to freely blossom. Bake these little gems for about 30 minutes. This recipe makes about 14 medium sized puffs.

Oh my, the aroma in this place is unbelievable. I wish you could be here with us. Mom's cream puffs have just emerged from the oven and I'm in love.

As soon as they come out of the oven, my Mom cuts a small slit in the side to let the steam out. Let them cool. She says don't touch. When they're completely cooled tuck them away in an airtight container.

Serving time... make a cut almost all the way through the puff. With lovingkindness and compassion fill each one with whipped cream, close them up lightly and tenderly drizzle with chocolate, caramel sauce or honey. Watch family and friends flock to your home.

Joy cometh! May you, like these dreamy creamy cream puffs, be filled with, "all joy and peace in believing, so that you will abound in hope by the power of the Holy Spirit." Romans 15:13!

Index

Where do I find that Recipe?

CPSIA information can be obtained at www.ICGtesting.com
Printed in the USA
242374LV00002B/7/P